Carreg Gwa

GREA
WALKS FROM
LLANBERIS

Des Marshall

LLANBERIS

Llyn Peris and Dinorwig quarry

First published in 2018

ISBN: 978-1-84524-278-7

Cover design: Carreg Gwalch
Cover image: Dolbadarn castle

Published by Gwasg Carreg Gwalch,
12 Iard yr Orsaf, Llanrwst, Wales LL26 0EH
tel: 01492 642031
email: books@carreg-gwalch.cymru
website: www.carreg-gwalch.cymru

Llyn Padarn, morning mist

Llyn Padarn from Snowdon's summit

Hazards and Problems
Take Notice, Take Care

The author and the publishers stress that walkers should be aware of the dangers that may occur on all walks.

- check local weather forecast before walking; do not walk up into mist or low clouds
- use local OS maps side by side with walking guides
- wear walking boots and clothing
- do not take any unnecessary risks – conditions can change suddenly and can vary from season to season
- take special care when accompanied by children or dogs
- when walking on roads, ensure that you are conspicuous to traffic from either direction

Contents

Introduction   7

1. Around Llyn Padarn   12
2. A Circuit of Vivian Quarry   18
3. An Exploration of Dinorwig Quarry   24
4. Ceunant Mawr (Llanberis Waterfall) and
   an Old Fort   30
5. Llyn Dwythwch   36
6. Dolbadarn Castle, Coed Victoria and Ceunant Mawr
   (Llanberis Waterfall)   40
7. To Dinorwig, a Slate Quarrying Village   46
8. Llanberis to Cwm y Glo Circular Walk   52
9. Moel Eilio via Bwlch y Groes   58
10. 'An alternative horseshoe', Moel Cynghorion,
    Foel Goch, Foel Gron and Moel Eilio   62
11. Snowdon by the Llanberis Path   68
12. Vivian Quarry and Dinorwig Quarry Hospital   74
13. Short Walks from Gilfach Ddu   78
14. Llyn Cwmffynnon   84
15. Around Nant Peris   88
16. Coed Dinorwig and a brief look at Dinorwig Quarry   92
17. The ascent of Cefn Du   98
18. Llyn Padarn View   104
19. Cei Llydan to Gilfach Ddu   108
20. Coed Doctor and Llyn Tomos Lewis   112
21. Coed Mawr   116
22. Llanberis, Cwm y Glo, Fachwen and back to
    Llanberis Circular Walk   120

Hafod Eryri at the summit of Snowdon

Introduction

Llanberis takes its name from St Peris, an early Christian, although the church he established was in the hamlet of Nant Peris, otherwise known as 'Old Llanberis'. Once connected to the railway Llanberis grew as the slate quarries developed.

The village is, perhaps, one of the main tourist centres in Snowdonia. In recent years the village has developed its' attractions such as the Snowdon Mountain Railway, Electric Mountain or even the Llanberis Lake Railway. The National Slate Museum along with the dive centre and adventurous rock climbing in Vivian Quarry close to Gilfach Ddu have all helped to put Llanberis on the map. One of the greatest rock climbing test pieces on slate is a fine technical climb called 'Come the Dervish' in Vivian Quarry.

Although it is possible to walk and climb the high mountain summits close by from Llanberis this guide details many of the excellent lower level walks that can be done from the village or near to. The mountain walks are well documented elsewhere for mountain walkers. However, I have chosen three mountain walks. One, the Llanberis Path up Snowdon can be approached and walked directly from the village and is also used as a basis for the second walk 'An Alternative Horseshoe', an uncrowded classic walk once the Llanberis Path is left behind. The third is a great introduction to mountain walking, the ascent of Moel Eilio. I have chosen not to include, for example, the Miner's or PYG tracks up Snowdon, the ascent of Glyder Fawr from Pen y Pass or Elidir Fawr and Y Garn from Nant Peris.

Walks in this guide have been chosen as some of the best in the area and cater for all abilities. The lakeside walks are suitable for wheelchair users. Many of the walks look at the history of the area especially in regard to the slate quarries whilst others explore fine oak woodlands. There are a couple of waterfall walks as well as one to a castle. Although there are other walks in the area I feel there is a good choice for all to enjoy at whatever level.

It will be noted that very few map references are given for the starts of most of the walks. That is because they start from easily found features in the village or just outside, for example Gilfach Ddu car park or Pen y Pass car park. Those that cannot be identified by features are given map references, for example Maen-llwyd-isaf. The furthest start is at Pen y Pass and the bus is best caught to the start of that walk because car parking there is limited and is always full from 08.00. The car park at the park and ride in Nant Peris is also often full from early in the morning.

As mentioned only three walks venture into high mountain terrain. That said many of the walks include mountainous terrain. As such it is important to dress accordingly and wear good, comfortable walking boots. Almost all the walks are exposed to sun and on hot days it is easy to dehydrate. Take plenty of water, food, a high factor sun screen and, daft as it might seem, an umbrella to provide shade when resting. In winter snow is always a threat when conditions high up become treacherous and a pair of crampons along with an ice axe will be necessary to ensure security. Needless to say the ability to stop yourself after you have had a slip by using an ice axe brake is mandatory. Take plenty of food, hot drink and spare clothing.

Gorffwysfa, Pen y Pass

Nant Peris

Another must have in your pack for the day is a group shelter. These come in different sizes from 4 man right up to 12 or more. They have saved many lives. A whistle is useful for summoning help after an incident and in winter a good head torch will help in finding your way down after nightfall. A basic first aid kit including any medicines needed for the day should also be taken.

Also important is to take the relevant map with you along with a compass although some people prefer using a GPS. That is fine so long as the battery is fully charged. The map for all these walks is the *Ordnance Survey 1:25,000 Explorer OL 17 Snowdon/Yr Wyddfa*. It is very important to know how to use these and for the not so technically minded a map and compass does not have to rely on batteries. Mobile phone signals are often hit and miss. In the event of an accident it may be necessary to find a point on the mountain where there is a signal. Always leave a note of where you are going and, importantly, at what time you expect to be back. If for some reason you do not get back home or to where you are staying at the stated time the rescue team can be alerted. When running behind schedule it is important that when you get down off the mountain let people know you are back at the car, or the nearest point having a signal to avoid an un-necessary rescue call out.

Historical and other notes regarding each individual walk are given in the walk description. Llanberis has several pubs, cafes, restaurants and outdoor shops as well as a few hotels and many B & B's. Unfortunately all the car parks are fee charging whilst parking in the village streets is very time limiting. Street parking close to the Mountain Railway is by resident permit.

Llanberis is now on the up and its revival is due to the influx of tourists and the attractions here. These have been developed since the closure of the slate quarries and mines. The Snowdon Mountain Railway has always been a big draw since 1896, although the first run was undertaken in 1895. Although the village has a bypass the High Street is much more pleasant to walk down and admire the shops or sample some of the local food. Llanberis is also on the 'Slate Trail' an 85 mile long walk connecting the major slate quarrying areas of Snowdonia.

The village and surrounding area draws people from all over the world time and time again. I hope during your visit and experiencing some of the walks inside this guide you will return again and again to complete them all. Happy walking!

Walk 1

Around Llyn Padarn

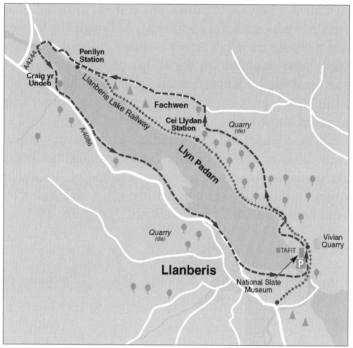

Llyn Padarn from the bridge at the end of Llyn Padarn

Walk details

Distance:	*5½ miles/8.8 kilometres*
Time (approx.):	*2½ hours*
Map:	*OS Explorer 1:25,000 OL17 Snowdon/Yr Wyddfa*
Start:	*The Gwynedd County Council fee paying car park at Gilfach Ddu*
Access:	*Directly from the car park*
Going:	*On obvious paths, tracks and roads following white ringed marker posts*

Walk description

This is a great walk with much of interest, history, including old quarry relics, fine woodland, a bubbling stream and fine views, not least up the whole length of Llyn Padarn towards Snowdon and Elidir Fawr. The walk follows white ringed marker posts although these sometimes disappear ...

Llyn Padarn is not particularly deep having a maximum depth of only 30 metres but is, however, the 6th deepest in Wales. Arctic Char, a species of fish dating back to the last Ice Age, is found here.

Starting from the sign for the Padarn lake walk at the far end of the car park by the ruins is a white ringed marker post. Follow the track to a fine viewpoint below the Quarry Hospital. Climb the steps up to this. If it is open it is well worth a visit. Bear left and pass the old mortuary dated 1906! Follow the white ringed marker posts, past an information panel and up to a viewpoint. Continue, quite steeply, through Coed Dinorwig

Llanberis, Llyn Peris and Llyn Padarn

Nant Fachwen

dominated by fine sessile oaks to another, but better, view point.

The view is quite extensive with Snowdon 1,085 metres visible. Above Llanberis are the lower mountains of, left to right, Moel Cynghorion 674 metres, Foel Goch 605 metres Foel Gron 629 metres and finally Moel Eilio 726 metres.

The path now descends and goes down steps to where it levels out. Continue down ignoring a turning down to the left to a gate just before a pretty stream, the Nant Fachwen.

An alternative goes down to the left from the ignored turning to the ruins of an old woollen mill and arrives at the footbridge of the parent walk.

Go through the gate and turn right. Cross the clapper bridge to where the path becomes a track. Go up this still following the white ringed marker posts. Continue through old quarry workings. The track becomes concrete and then tarmac as it climbs steadily to a right hand bend. Leave the track here by a marker post. Walk up the short section of path and through a gate to join a narrow road.

Turn left and pass a phone box – no phone!! Follow the road down through Fachwen to reach the end of the lake. The road bears left to reach a 'T' junction. Turn left over the fine bridge but before doing so there is a metal plaque to the left on which is a lovely poem written by Gillian Clarke.

But for how?
Cherish these mountains, born in fire and ash
out of the sea to make this wilderness,
asleep for aeons beneath ice and snow,
carved by the shifting glaciers long ago,
till ten millennia back, the last ice age
made right for fern and purple saxifrage
this place whose evolution's given birth
to the rare Snowdon Lily's home on earth
but all could go with the melting snow

The view up Llyn Padarn from the bridge is superb. On the left is Elidir Fawr 924 metres and Snowdon on the right.

Turn left at the end of the bridge along an old section of road and continue through a pair of gates. Go past Craig yr Undeb to join the main road, the A4086, after passing through two more gates in quick succession.

Craig yr Undeb – Union Rock – was the secret meeting point for quarrymen who wanted to set up a union. The quarry owners were dead against that idea. However, in the 1870's 110 quarrymen declared that they were in fact going to be union members. They were instantly

Carreg yr Undeb (Union Rock)

locked out by Captain Wallace Cragg, the owner of Glynrhonwy Quarry. Realising that he was losing too much money the quarrymen were reinstated 3 weeks later and regarded as union members. *The quarry owners refused permission to hold meetings both in the quarries and on land owned by the estates. Lord Newborough of the Glynllifon estate allowed the men to use Craig yr Undeb. Out of these meetings the North Wales Quarrymen's Union was created in 1874.*

Turn left alongside the road for 150 metres to a gap in the wall on the left. Go through this and descend to the track bed of the old railway.

Note the old railway tunnel to the right. This track was part of the main line to Llanberis that closed in 1969.

Follow the track bed of the old railway line to reach a barrier. Pass this to arrive at toilets on the right. Turn left and down then almost immediately turn right. Follow the waymarked path into a rough car park then bear up to the access

The bridge at the end of Llyn Padarn

road. Turn left to reach the A4086 once again.

Turn left. Continue alongside the road until just before the Gwynedd County Council car park signed for the village. The path bears left down to the lake side and continues alongside it to arrive at a children's play area. Pass to the right of this into another car park and bear left again towards the lake.

Follow this path and go over a footbridge. Continue across the field, or by the water's edge, to another footbridge. Go through the gate and cross the bridge, noting the bridge for the Llanberis Lake Railway over to the right, to reach the access road for the Slate Museum and Gilfach Ddu car park. Turn left along the path by the road to the car park.

The Llanberis Lake Railway has a track gauge of 1'11½" along 2 miles of track along the shore of Llyn Padarn on part of the old track-bed of the slate railway to Porth Dinorwig. This makes a very gentle and worthwhile journey alongside Llyn Padarn.

Elidir Fawr and Llyn Padarn at sunrise

Walk 2

A Circuit of Vivian Quarry

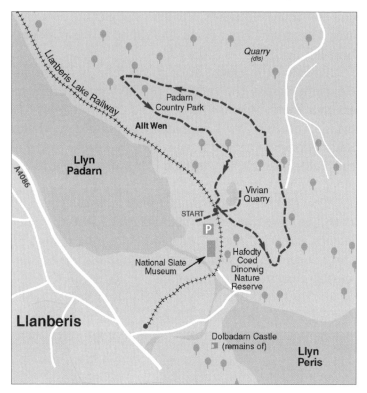

View over Llanberis to Glynrhonwy slate quarries

Walk details

Distance:	*1¾ miles/2.8 kilometres*
Time (approx.):	*2 hours*
Map:	*OS Explorer 1:25,000 OL17 Snowdon/Yr Wyddfa*
Start:	*The Gwynedd County Council fee paying car park at Gilfach Ddu*
Access:	*Directly from the car park*
Please note:	*The paths are often steep in ascent and very steep on descent with irregular steps where care is needed especially in wet weather*
Going:	*On obvious paths or tracks*

Walk description

This is a great walk taking in the flooded pit of Vivian Quarry part of the A1 incline and several drum houses. The walk from the upper one is through fine sessile oak woodland floored with bluebells in spring. A visit to Anglesey Barracks is a stark reminder of how the quarrymen lived and worked. There is a great view of the surrounding mountains, Llanberis and Llyn Padarn from the top of the incline before going into the woodland.

Walk out of the car park towards the Llanberis Lake Railway. Cross the line and continue to the dive centre. Pass through the fine arch to the right into Vivian Quarry. Follow the path to a viewing platform where divers below and climbers above are often seen. Note the 'Blondin' dangling over the water.

A part of the gigantic Dinorwig Quarry work in Vivian

'Blondin' in Vivian Quarry

Quarry ceased in 1958. It shared all the facilities of Dinorwig but was classed as separate from it. The water is around 18 metres (60 feet) deep.

Blondins are specialised forms of Chain Inclines. They allow loads to be picked up and transported and set down at any point along it.

Slate had many uses and apart from the obvious ones of slates for roofs and as building material it was used for the beds for snooker tables, cosmetics, building roads, walls, fences, homeopathic remedies, gravestones and cisterns. All the best snooker tables apparently have slate beds! Slate from the Llanberis quarries was exported worldwide.

Return through the arch and turn left up the side of the cleaned A1 incline. Where the 'cleaned' section ends continue up the 'uncleaned' section to the drum house seen at the top. *There is a fine example of the braking mechanism as well as the drum.* Keep following the incline steeply up to another but much more ruinous one. Continue below the drum and footbridge. Turn left immediately beyond this and go up to a marker post.

Going over the footbridge to the start of a fine walled path there are superb views of the mountains, Llanberis

Llanberis, Llyn Padarn and Moel Eilio from near top of quarry

and Llyn Padarn. The mountains are from left to right, Moel Cynghorion 674 metres, Foel Goch 605 metres, Foel Gron 629 metres and the massive looking Moel Eilio 726 metres.

Return over the bridge and continue up the path through very fine sessile oak woodland a part of the Dinorwig Nature Reserve.

Bluebells carpet the ground in spring.

Continue up to a path that goes off to the right. Turn right here to view Anglesey Barracks. Return to the path and continue steeply up to reach a level track going off to the right. Ignore this. Go up to the left and continue up to go through a gap in a low wall. Turn left and pass an information panel. Follow the level path to where it rises again and passes above the impressive gash of Vivian Quarry.

There are more amazing views of Llanberis and mountains including Snowdon 1,085 metres.

Continue along and up to reach a track.

Anglesey Barracks

Turn left along it, a part of the old tramway. On a low wall before a higher one is a fine circular etching. Turn left 100 metres beyond the low wall where there is a marker post. Follow the path down keeping the fence to the left to a kissing gate. Pass through this and follow the path to the right and go over a ladder stile. Continue to a 'T' junction. Turn left and down. Marker posts lower down confirm the correct way has been taken! At the 'Y' junction turn left, as indicated by the marker post, and continue down through more fine sessile oak woodland. Continue straight ahead at the red topped marker post. At the next path junction go up to the left and then go along to a drum house. Continue above it on a level path to the edge of Vivian Quarry,

Descend a series of very steep and irregular slate steps, CARE especially in wet weather. At the base of these bear left at marker posts and descend 3 more series of very steep slate steps again taking care. At the top of the third set there is a fine view of the quarry. Climbers can often be seen gathered on the ledges, usually in summer, contemplating their next moves! Descend more steps to a reach a level track. Turn left and pass ruins. Continue down past another great view of the quarry again and descend an easier angled set of steps to reach a road.

Going right leads up to the quarry hospital.

Turn left down the road then turn right through a gap in the wall 25 metres further. Descend yet more steps to reach the rear of the Llanberis Lake Railway café and ticket office. Turn left then right to return to the car park.

Walk 3

An Exploration of Dinorwig Quarry

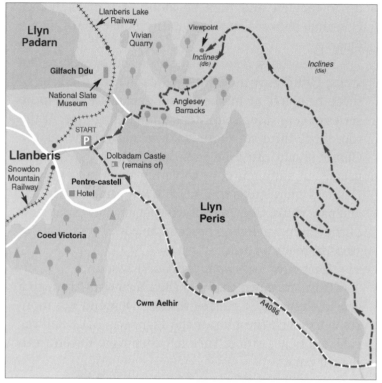

View looking down the zigzag path

Walk details

Distance:	*4¼ miles/6.8 kilometres*
Time (approx.):	*3 hours*
Map:	*OS Explorer 1:25,000 OL17 Snowdon/Yr Wyddfa*
Start:	*The Gwynedd County Council fee paying car park for Dolbadarn castle*
Access:	*Turn down the road opposite the Snowdon Mountain Railway signed for the Llanberis Lake Railway and National Slate Museum. The car park is on the left 200 metres down this road*
Please note:	*Do not enter any of the workings*
Going:	*On obvious paths or tracks with a section along the road after visiting Dolbadarn castle, fortunately along a wide footpath*

Walk description

This is a superb walk that traverses one of the largest slate quarries in Wales. It beggars belief that everything seen on the spoil heaps has been put there by human endeavour. The huge pit of Matilda Quarry is truly spectacular and the many inclines are a testimony to the quarrymen's ingenuity. Views of the surrounding mountains are spectacular as well as ones to Llanberis and Llyn Padarn. Part of the Dinorwig Nature Reserve, with fine sessile oaks, is descended past the Anglesey barracks to follow an amazing walled path down to the road. A visit is made to Dolbadarn castle before walking along the A4086 on a good footpath close to the start.

Walk out of the car park to the road and cross over. Turn left then right almost immediately across the footbridge. Continue up the roughly tarmacked path and climb a short flight of steps to reach a wall. Pass through the gap by the side of the stone hut and continue up to the castle. Return to the gap and turn left before it. Follow the path to a 'Y' junction. Follow the left arm of the 'Y' on a good and clearer path descending slightly to go through a kissing gate to a track. Turn right up this to reach the A4086. Turn left and follow it passing a car park in a large loop of the old road on the right.

The enormity of the quarry workings can be appreciated when walking along the road.

Continue along the footpath beyond the car park towards Nant Peris for 250 metres to an access road with a bridleway finger post. Turn left through the gate

The zigzag path

and follow the tarmac road to reach a 'Y' junction. Go up the left arm of the 'Y' and pass through a kissing gate at the start of a rough track where the tarmac ends.

Looking down on Dolbadarn castle

Follow the track up as it steepens by the first spoil heap. Continue up to where it levels briefly.

This is New York Level.

The track swings right and goes up less steeply.

Up to the right forming the skyline is Crib Goch.

When the track switchbacks left there is a fine view of Moel Eilio 726 metres. Continue 'a zigging and a zagging' up through this incredible and ruinous landscape to a huge deep pit. Pass between high walls and continue along a level track to where it descends slightly into a dip.

There is a hidden quarry pool, although often just a muddy or dry hollow, to the right beyond the substantial fencing!

Go up to where the track levels and bears left.

Note the fine incline going up to the right.

Continue to a kissing gate. Pass through this.

Note the ruined large mill over to the right.

Turn left and continue along the very wide track to a superb view point.

The mountains forming the skyline are left to right, Crib y Ddysgl 1,065 metres at the end of Crib Goch and close to the summit of Snowdon which it hides. To the right

Remains of Drumhouse

is Moel Cynghorion 674 metres, Foel Goch 605 metres, Foel Gron 629 metres and Moel Eilio.

Return to the kissing gate just passed through and turn right immediately in front of it through another. The path bears right and continues down the straight incline with a fence to the left and passes between high slate walls. Carry on down. *Note the frequent holes in the slate that housed the holding brackets for the incline rails as well as lengths of the 'I' section line, the rollers and occasional lengths of wire.*

Pass between more walls to where the path levels and reaches a drum house. Bear right then step through a low wall and pass to the right of the house. Turn left and keep following the fence down passing several blue ringed marker posts to where it is possible

Quarry features

to turn right through a wide doorway to view Anglesey Barracks.

Return to the path and continue down the incline to where it levels and bears right. Carry on until below an ancient metal footbridge with a ruined drum house just beyond it. Go up to the right immediately before going underneath the bridge to a clear path. Turn left across the bridge to the start of a remarkable walled path. Follow this down to where it leaves it to descend a steep slope interspersed with irregular slate steps and a final short section of walled path to reach the road. Turn right to the roundabout then turn left and follow the footpath back to the car park.

Assheton-Smith the landowner started slate quarrying here in 1782. By the turn of the century there were 13 levels some 18 – 23 metres high. The first incline was built in 1789 but sledges were more often used until 1816. One of the features of Dinorwig Quarry were the 2 main inclines. These had many sections or pitches. Each pitch would connect 2 or perhaps 3 terraces. Steam locomotives arrived in the 1870's with petrol ones arriving in 1930. There were some 50 miles of railway lines and 15 miles of compressed air pipes. The main mill was on a level with Dinorwig village and is best seen when walking back from the viewpoint. 'Blondins' were installed in the 1930's and electric power came from Cwm Dyli in 1905. The quarry's output in the late 1890's was 100,000 tons per annum. When you think that would have produced a million tons of waste to be scattered over the slopes of Elidir Fawr! Almost 3,000 workers were employed at that time. Work stopped in 1969.

An incline wall

Walk 4

Ceunant Mawr (Llanberis Waterfall) and an Old Fort

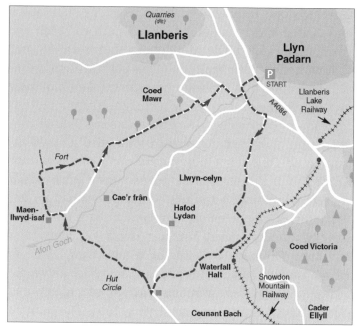

Llanberis, Elidir Fawr and Y Garn

Walk details

Distance: *3 miles/4.8 kilometres*

Time (approx.):   *2½ hours*

Map: *OS Explorer 1:25,000 OL17 Snowdon/Yr Wyddfa*

Start: *The Gwynedd County Council fee paying car park for the Village and Electric Mountain*

Access: *This car park is signed Village car park and Electric Mountain*

Please note: *Take care when crossing the Snowdonia Mountain Railway line to view the falls and do not trespass on the railway. The upper part of the falls, reached from the second access point, are easily seen without any need to go nearer to the long drop!*

Going: *On obvious paths or tracks with short sections of very quiet road walking*

Walk description

This is a great walk with much of interest including the Snowdon Mountain Railway, Llanberis Waterfall, expansive views to Snowdon, across Llanberis to Dinorwig Quarry on Elidir Fawr and an old fort. Although only the top of the waterfall is visible it is a fine view of it. To view the base of the fall Walk 6 is a great way to do this as it also visits Dolbadarn castle and a fine woodland.

Walk out of the car park past an information panel and the children's play area to the road. Cross this and up the short access road signed to the village centre to the High Street. Turn left. Continue past the

The top waterfall

Dolbadarn and Padarn Lake Hotels to Snowdon Garage. Cross the road to this and up the road immediately before it.

The garage offers a fee paying car parking facility accessed from the quiet road.

Continue up to a white cottage on the left. Immediately beyond it is a finger post by some steps.

Turn right up these and through a gate. Continue up the flight of steps straight ahead. At the top of these go through a gate (or gap if the gate is off its' hinges). Carry on and pass to the right of a property then up to and through a kissing gate. Keep going up to reach a track.

There is a great view of Dinorwig Quarry and Elidir Fawr 924 metres here.

Follow the track to a narrow tarmacked lane. Turn right up this. Just past the cottage on the right is a kissing gate on the left. Pass through this and cross the line carefully to a fine viewpoint of Ceunant Mawr. Return to the lane and turn left up it. At the junction with a track on the left there is another kissing gate over to the left. Go through this and cross the line carefully to view the fine upper waterfall.

CARE needs to be taken here as there is a high cliff down to the left. The waterfall is easily seen without recourse to any scrambling to get closer.

Return to the lane and turn left up to a waymarked kissing gate on the left below a wood chalet at a sharp right hand bend. Go through this and follow the grassy path with a wall to the right to a hidden kissing gate also on the right. Ignore this. Continue straight ahead to an obvious 'Y' junction 10 metres ahead. Go up the right hand arm of the 'Y' again with a wall to the right and up to another kissing gate immediately beyond a tiny stream. Pass through the gate and with the stream to the left continue up the edge of the stony field to the access track into Hafod Uchaf, the building on the left and a narrow lane.

There is a bail out option here by turning right and following the lane down to Llanberis.

Go up the tarmacked lane to go through a gate. Turn right on to a track signed as a bridleway. Go over the ladder stile or more easily through the gate. Follow the track up to another ladder stile and gate.

There is a great view of Snowdon 1,085 metres here.

Again it is easier to go through the gate! Continue along the track to cross a footbridge over the Afon Goch. Go up the track with the wall to the right to a narrow tarmacked lane. Turn left up to some ruins, Maen-llwyd-isaf.

Another bail out option is available here by turning right on reaching the narrow lane back down to Llanberis.

Continue up past these on the diminishing tarmac then follow the grassy track up to a gate and ladder stile. Again it is easier through the gate! At the 'Y' junction just ahead go right then right again 25 metres further on a narrow path. Continue to an old kissing gate on the right. Ignore this for now and continue up the short but steep slope, with the wall to the right, to the summit adorned with a crude stone shelter.

There is a great view from here and is well worth the effort. Beyond Llanberis is Dinorwig Quarry, Elidir Fawr, Y Garn 947 metres and Glyder Fawr 1,001 metres.

The cairn on top of the viewpoint

Snowdon is very prominent whilst below and right of it is Moel Cynghorion 674 metres and right again almost above here is Moel Eilio 726 metres.

Return to the old kissing gate and pass through it. Follow the path down to go through a more recent kissing gate. The path continues down through bracken and gorse and is quite steep at times to reach a narrow tarmac lane. Turn left down this towards Llanberis. At the 'T' junction beyond the first houses turn right then left 25 metres further. Continue down to the next 'T' junction and turn right to go down to the High Street arriving opposite The Heights. Turn left then right 50 metres further opposite the Spar and go down the lane back to the car park.

The possibility of building a railway to the top of Snowdon 1,085 metres (3,560ft) was proposed as early as 1869. The landowner at that time, Assheton-Smith of the Vaynol Estate, was set against it believing it would spoil the view. It was not until December 1894 that the first sod was cut! Assheton-Smith had acceded and the sod was cut by his daughter Enid, pronounced Ennid. Locomotive No 2 was named after her. The line was completed in February 1896 and cost £63,800. In today's terms that equates to around £6,658,000!

Incredibly by April 1895 50% of the earth works had been completed. Tracklaying had to start at one end to enable the rack to be correctly aligned. As such this did not start until August 1895. Progress was rapid as locomotives were able to ferry the equipment up the line. It is quite remarkable in view of the often dire weather that the line was laid to the summit by January 1896. The steepest gradient is 1:5.5.

The 4.7 miles (7.5 kilometres) railway with a gauge of 2' 7 ½" (800mm) was opened on Easter Monday 1896. Colonel Sir Francis Marindin from the Board of Trade had previously inspected the line on the 27th March. Everything worked well and his only recommendation was that the wind speed be monitored and if too strong trains to be stopped. Carriages are always uphill of the locomotive and, as on that first run, not coupled to it. This is an important feature. On the descent that Easter Monday the engine, No 1 L.A.D.A.S., disengaged form the track and plunged over a cliff. Fortunately the driver and fireman were able to jump clear. The braking system on the carriages allowed them to safely come to a halt. Unfortunately two passengers seeing that the driver and fireman had leapt to safety also leapt from the train with one of them sustaining fatal injuries.

Because of this the line was closed for a year until flanged guard rails were installed each side of the rack rails. These keep the train engaged to the track if a carriage or locomotive starts to mount the running rails and gives constant traction throughout the whole journey.

Trains usually run from mid-March through October. Early and late in the season trains may not go all the way stopping at Clogwyn and bad weather may prevent trains running at all. Trains are not time tabled but the first train leaves Llanberis at 09.00 and continues as long as there is demand. It takes about an hour for the train to reach the summit.

Walk 5

Llyn Dwythwch

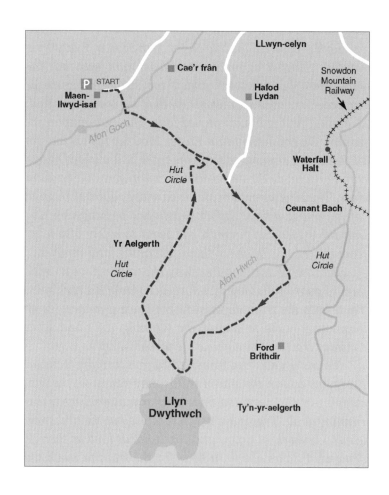

Walk details

Distance:	*2½ miles/4 kilometres*
Time (approx.):	*1¾ hours*
Map:	*OS Explorer 1:25,000 OL17 Snowdon/Yr Wyddfa*
Start:	*The car parking area at Maen-llwyd-isaf. Grid reference: SH 567594*
Access:	*From Llanberis turn up the road opposite The Heights – Ffordd Tŷ Du/Tŷ Du Road. Turn left 130 metres further. At the 'T' junction 160 metres further turn right then left 25 metres further again. Continue up the narrow road to where the tarmac ends by the ruins of Maen-llwyd-isaf*
Please note:	*After wet weather there are some boggy sections but are easily walked across*
Going:	*Other than the boggy ground the walking is on a good track*

Walk description

This quite scenic walk visits a seldom seen lake being completely hidden from view other than from the mountains above. It feels remote but there is often the reassuring sound of the Snowdon Mountain Railway chugging away in the background. Although boggy by the lake it is a good walk. It can be started from Llanberis but I think it is better to drive to the car parking area to avoid walking up the road.

Walk back down the road to the finger post indicating a bridleway. Turn right down this to reach a footbridge spanning the Afon Goch. Go through the

Llyn Dwythwch and Foel Goch

gate and cross the bridge. Continue along the track to another gate. This has a ladder stile to the left of it and it is much easier to go through the gate! Keep following the track through another gate ignoring the ladder stile and down to the end of a tarmac lane.

Ignore the gate on the lane to the left. Follow the rough track ahead gradually down to the bridge spanning the pretty Afon Hwch, the outflowing stream of Llyn Dwythwch. Pass through the gate. Ignoring the gate and ladder stile to the left go up to the top of the short rise. A very rough track branches right here. Turn right up this to where it fades and disappears. Bear very slightly right across boggy ground to a fence where another track appears.

Follow the track on the left of the fence to where it too degenerates to reach a ladder stile on the right by the water's edge.

This is a very tranquil place surrounded by the mountains.

Possibly Dwythwch was once Gwythwch taken from

Elidir Fawr, Y Garn and Dinorwig slate quarry

gwyddwch meaning a wild male goat. It could also describe the streams that pour into the lake. Local legend claim this is one of the sites to see the 'Tylwyth Teg' or faeries dancing, another being Llyn y Gadair at Rhyd-ddu.

Climb over the stile and go diagonally right across boggy ground to reach a faint path. Turn right along this to join a track.

There is a great view of Elidir Fawr 924 metres, Y Garn 947 metres, Glyder Fawr 1,001 metres, Crib y Ddysgl 1,065 metres, Snowdon 1,085 metres, Moel Cynghorion 674 metres, Foel Goch 605 metres and Foel Gron 629 metres. The steep slope rising to the right of the lake is that of Moel Eilio 726 metres.

Continue along this to where it descends to a gate with a ladder stile on the right. Once more it is easier to go through the gate. Continue down to join the track of the outward walk. Turn left up this back to the car parking area.

Walk 6

Dolbadarn Castle, Coed Victoria and Ceunant Mawr (Llanberis Waterfall)

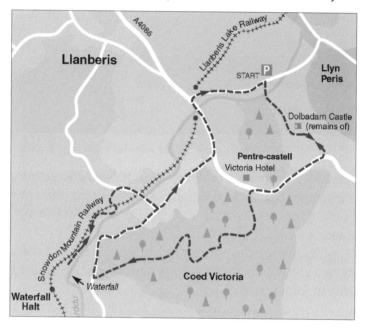

Dolbadarn castle

Walk details

Distance:	*2½ miles/4 kilometres*
Time (approx.):	*2 hours*
Map:	*OS Explorer 1:25,000 OL17 Snowdon/Yr Wyddfa*
Start:	*The Gwynedd County Council fee paying car park for Dolbadarn castle*
Access:	*Turn down the road opposite the Snowdon Mountain Railway signed for the Llanberis Lake Railway and National Slate Museum. The car park is on the left 200 metres down this road*
Please note:	*The very narrow spiral staircase ascending the keep at Dolbadarn castle is very steep as well as having no handrail. If ascending and descending this be very careful*
	Do not venture further than the end of the path at the waterfall. The ground above it is very steep, wet and insecure
Going:	*On obvious paths or tracks with short sections of road walking*

Walk description

This is a lovely and quite easy walk taking in the finely sited Dolbadarn castle a lovely section of woodland and a pretty waterfall. The time given could well be exceeded due to spending time looking at the views.

Dolbadarn castle was built in the early 1200's by Llywelyn ap Iowerth (otherwise known as Llywelyn the Great). It was a stamp of his authority of power in the area. Of simple design it pre-dates the fortifications of

Edward I during construction of his colonial castles. The impressive remnant of the keep stands over 15 metres high and was considered by the historian Richard Avent as 'the finest surviving example of a Welsh round tower'.

Llywelyn ap Iorwerth died in 1240. His grandson Llywelyn ap Gruffudd (or 'Llywelyn the Last Leader') gained control over Gwynedd by imprisoning his brother Owain Goch for over 20 years in the tower. After Llywelyn ap Gruffudd died his other brother Dafydd ap Gruffudd tried to maintain independence from English rule. Unfortunately Edward I captured the castle in 1283 and set about ruling Wales and building his castle in Caernarfon. The castle itself was plundered for its stone and wooden beams to help build the one in Caernarfon. Many artists have painted Dolbadarn castle, not least J. M. W. Turner (1775 – 1851) between 1798 and 1799.

Walk out of the car park to the road and cross over.

View from the spiral staircase towards Llyn Padarn

Turn left then right almost immediately across the footbridge. Continue up the roughly tarmacked path and climb a short flight of steps to reach a wall. Pass through the gap by the side of the stone hut and turn up to the right. Walk up the grass slope with a wall to the right to where an easy path leads up to the tower and steps leading up the side of it. Climb these to view the inside. For the sure footed it is possible to climb the very steep and narrow, stone, spiral staircase to the top. Return to the grassy area and go past the place where you turned. Go straight ahead and down to join another path. Turn left along this and descend slightly. Continue to go through a kissing gate to a track. Turn right up this to reach the A4086.

Turn right down the footpath by the side of the road and follow it for 300 metres until just before the Royal Victoria Hotel. Across the road a finger post, gate and ladder stile is seen. Cross carefully over to these.

Climb over the ladder stile and follow the path/track through Coed Victoria. Pass through a kissing gate and continue on the path gradually up and then along through a gap in the fence. Continue and pass through another kissing gate. The path passes between a wall on the left and a fence on the right to reach a gate by the Pen y Ceunant tea rooms.

Go through the gate to the very narrow minor road and turn right down the steep road. Pass through the gate to the right of the cattle grid and continue to a road junction at a black finger post. Turn

Small waterfall on the way to view the lower part of Llanberis waterfall

left as indicated on the finger post to the waterfall. Continue along the road and pass under the viaduct of the Snowdon Mountain Railway. Ignore the right turning to Dôl Elidir Blaen Ddôl and continue along the road that bears left. Turn left 50 metres further on at the sign for the waterfall.

Llanberis waterfall from the end of the path

Go through the kissing gate and walk up the lane with a fence on the left. Turn left again when the fence bears left. Follow the path on the right of this. There is no sign here and the path easy to miss. Follow the path, passing under the railway viaduct again, to reach the Afon Arddu. Continue on the path on the right of the river passing some small waterfalls to reach the fine main waterfall. Retrace steps to the black finger post beyond which is a row of terraced houses, Vaynol Terrace 1906. Turn left and continue down the road to the main road. Turn left to the terminus of the Snowdon Mountain Railway. Cross the road and turn right down the road to the car park.

Dinorwig quarry from Dolbadarn castle

Walk 7

To Dinorwig, a Slate Quarrying Village

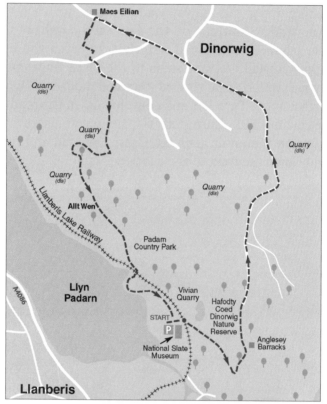

The upper part of Nant Fachwen

Walk details

Distance: *3¼ miles/5.2 kilometres*

Time (approx.): *2½ hours*

Map: *OS Explorer 1:25,000 OL17 Snowdon/Yr Wyddfa*

Start: *The Gwynedd County Council fee paying car park at Gilfach Ddu*

Access: *Directly from the car park*

Please note: *Do not enter any of the quarry remains*

Going: *On obvious paths, tracks or roads*

Walk description

This is a great walk taking in the flooded pit of Vivian Quarry, part of the A1 incline and several drum houses. The walk from the upper one is through fine sessile oak woodland which is floored with vast numbers of bluebells in spring. The Anglesey Barracks are a stark reminder of how the quarrymen lived and worked. There is a great view of the surrounding mountains, Llanberis and Llyn Padarn from the top of the incline before going into the woodland again. Having walked through the village there is a very fine view from the descent path before following the lovely Nant Fachwen down to a slate bridge where white ringed marker posts are followed back to the start.

Walk out of the car park towards the Llanberis Lake Railway. Cross the line and continue to the dive centre. Pass through the fine arch to the right into Vivian Quarry. Follow the path to a viewing platform

where divers below and climbers above are often seen.
Note the 'Blondin' cableway suspended above and the remarkable terracing, known as galleries, in the quarry.

Return through the arch and turn left up the side of the A1 incline to where the cleaned section ends. Continue up the 'uncleaned section' to the drum house seen at the top where there is a fine example of the braking mechanism as well as the drum. Keep following the incline steeply up to another but much more ruinous one. Continue below the drum of this and the footbridge. Turn left immediately after passing below the bridge and go up to a marker post.

Assheton-Smith the landowner started slate quarrying here in 1782. By the turn of the century there were 13 levels some 18 – 23 metres high. The first incline was built in 1789 but sledges were more often used until 1816. One of the features of Dinorwig Quarry were the 2 main inclines. These had many sections or pitches. Each pitch would connect 2 or perhaps 3 terraces. Steam locomotives arrived in the 1870's with petrol ones arriving in 1930. There were some 50 miles of railway lines and 15 miles of compressed air pipes. The main mill was on a level with Dinorwig village.

'Blondins' were installed in the 1930's and electric power came from Cwm Dyli in 1905. The quarry's output in the late 1890's was 100,000 tons per annum. When you think that 1 ton of usable slate was obtained from 10 tons of quarried material would have produced almost a million tons of waste to be scattered over the slopes of Elidir Fawr! Almost 3,000 workers were employed at that time. Work stopped in 1969.

Turn right. Follow the path up through very fine sessile oak woodland, a part of Coed Dinorwig and the Nature Reserve. Continue up to where a path goes off to the right. Turn right here to view the Anglesey Barracks. Return to the path and continue up, steeply, to reach a level track going off to the right. Turn right

Inscription on the Quarrymen's Memorial

along this, ignoring the path going up to the left. Continue up the track to a terrace of small cottages. Just past these the track becomes a tarmacked road by the Blue and White Peris Outdoor Centre. Continue along the road to a large looping layby on the right.

Note the memorial to the quarrymen on the right.

Keep following the road through the village and go past a café. This is a great one and well worth stopping for a cuppa and snack. They also have a selection of books for sale and some cards. Continue past this to a bus stop and shelter on the left. Immediately beyond this is a kissing gate. Turn left through this and follow the path down to another kissing gate. There is a superb view down here.

The mountains forming the skyline are left to right, Crib y Ddysgl 1,065 metres at the end of Crib Goch ridge and Snowdon 1,085 metres. To the right are Moel Cynghorion 674 metres, Foel Goch 605 metres, Foel Gron 629 metres and Moel Eilio 726 metres towering above Llanberis nestling on the shore of Llyn Padarn.

Keep following the path down to a narrow road. Cross straight over down the dead end road. Turn right 200 metres further down at the end of a low white

The upper Nant Fachwen

The log bridge across the Nant Fachwen

cottage and follow the concreted strip access track down to a sharp right hand bend. On the left is a sign indicating the path that continues straight ahead. Continue, as indicated, up this to an old metal gate. There is s symbol here for the 'Pilgrim's Way'. Pass through the gate and follow the path to an old metal footbridge spanning Nant Fachwen. Cross this and continue along to where the path turns right in front of a gate with a green panel indicating the Padarn Country Park.

Descend easily at first following yellow ringed marker posts then down a series of intermittent steps to Nant Fachwen. This is very pretty indeed at this point. Cross the log floored footbridge, slippery when wet, and descend past the end of a low wall. Keep going down to a kissing gate.

Go through this to a track. Turn left down this to the slate bridge spanning the stream.

The spoil heap above the loop layby

Go across the bridge and bear right through a gate. Go up to the left at the path junction here and climb gradually up. In wet weather this is slippery. At the path junction with a path coming up from the right keep going to where the path levels at a small clearing and vantage point.

There is a great view from here similar to the one after leaving the road by the bus stop.

The path now starts to descend and reaches a 'Y' junction by point 4! Go right and down below ruins. Keep descending to a level section which leads to the Quarry Hospital after passing the mortuary dated 1906! The hospital is well worth a visit when open. There are also great views from here. Go down the steps in front of the hospital to a grassy area overlooking Llyn Padarn. Follow the path around and down to a path junction at a multi-coloured marker post. Either go straight ahead to the station or follow the marker posts to the car park.

Walk 8

Llanberis to Cwm y Glo Circular Walk

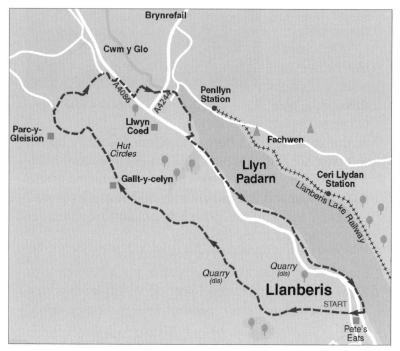

Deiniolen from the summit of the road

Walk details

Distance:	*5½ miles*
Time (approx.):	*3½ hours*
Map:	*OS Explorer 1:25,000 OL17 Snowdon/Yr Wyddfa*
Start:	*Goodman Street, Llanberis. This is opposite Pete's Eats*
Access:	*From any of the car parks in the village*
Please note:	*Do not venture into the mine workings. Take care when crossing the two busy roads*
Going:	*On roads, tracks or clearly followed paths*

Walk description

Although this walk is predominantly on a quiet road or abandoned railway track bed it is a fine scenic one. No boggy ground to worry about on this walk! Views are superb from the high point on the road. The final section from the end of the railway tunnel follows the last part of the Llyn Padarn circular walk following white ringed marker posts with fine views across Llyn Padarn.

Walk up Goodman Street, which is initially quite steep, ignoring all turnings, continue to where the road levels. Walk past the gate and information panel for Coed Doctor. After the house on the left, Ael y Bryn, keep following the road and pass a ruin seen to the left of the road.

This is all that remains of the early 17th century house built by the Dean of Westminster, Dr Goodman. Later he bequeathed it in order to help establish Christ's Hospital in Ruthin.

Continue along the pretty road to the spoil heaps of Glynrhonwy slate quarry. The road rises and passes between two very impressive pits. The pit on the left has some pinnacles whilst the one on the right has a deep looking black pool

The Glynrhonwy quarries closed in 1930. Between 1940 and 1943 during the Second World War they were requisitioned by the Air Ministry to store over 18,000 tons of bombs and explosives. Subsequently the quarries were used for bomb disposal. This continued up to 1956. However, it was not until 1975 that the site was cleared and declared safe and free from explosives. The left hand quarry was used as a venue by Ron Howard for the film 'Willow' starring Val Kilmer in 1968.

Developed in the 1870's the site incorporated several small scratchings. There was a large mill and a rail system on several levels. The quarry was one of the pioneers installing internal rail systems. It was the largest undertaking on the eastern side of the valley. In 1883 some 1,789 tons were produced when 70 men were employed. Later output increased to around 40 tons per man per year.

Looking back from here Snowdon 1,085 metres can be seen.

The road undulates, but generally rises, to reach the high point.

Just before reaching this on the right and just below a lone and large hawthorn small stone rings can be seen. These are the remains of Iron Age round huts that were sited here some 2,000 years ago.

The view from the high point is very good. Anglesey is spread out with Holyhead Mountain 220 metres on the far horizon. Puffin Island to the right is also prominent. Llyn

Padarn covers the valley floor with the cluster of houses above it, Deiniolen, looking like an Andalusian village. To the right is Elidir Fawr 924 metres, Y Garn 947 metres and Glyder Fawr 1,001 metres. The gash of Llanberis Pass with the road snaking up it, splits these mountains to those on the right. These are the pinnacles of Crib Goch, Crib y Ddysgl 1,065 metres and finally the pyramidal shaped summit of Snowdon 1,085 metres.

The road now descends quite steeply and a tree lined reservoir is seen ahead. When the road levels there is a finger post on the right at the junction of a good track signed Lon Bwlch. Turn right down this and follow the track as it passes between houses and descends to a finger post and steps on the right where the track swings 90 degrees to the left. Turn right down the steps. Descend the path with a tiny stream on the left to where the path becomes enclosed and continues to a narrow road. Walk down this to the road through the village. Turn right to reach the A4086. Turn right along the roadside path to where it ends. On the small cliff face to the right is a plaque commemorating an accident hereabouts.

One of the most dreadful accidents to happen in the area occurred on Wednesday 30th June 1869. It was a very hot day. Two carts carrying nitro-glycerine, to be used in the Glynrhonwy quarries, exploded. Five people and two horses were killed instantly. Another 8 were seriously injured with one of them dying a few days later. The explosion was so fierce that it created two craters 10 feet deep and 30 feet wide! Not a house within a mile radius was left unscathed. No trace was found of either the horses or two of the men. Some human remains were found a mile away and a wheel from one of the carts was found on the road close to the summit of the road previously walked!

Cross the road, carefully, onto the path at the far side and turn right along it to the sign for Y Fricsan. Turn left and walk up to a 'T' junction. Y Fricsan is up to the left. Turn right and follow the path to another main road the A4244. Cross this carefully and walk straight ahead down to the end of a pretty bridge at the end of Llyn Padarn. Keep going straight ahead to go through two gates in quick succession. Continue to Craig y Undeb.

Craig yr Undeb, Union Rock, was the secret meeting point for quarrymen who wanted to set up a union. The quarry owners were dead against that idea. However, in the 1870's 110 quarrymen declared that they were in fact going to be union members. They were instantly locked out by Captain Wallace Cragg, the owner of Glynrhonwy Quarry. Realising that he was losing too much money the quarrymen were reinstated 3 weeks later and regarded as union members. The quarry owners refused permission to hold meetings both in the quarries and on land owned by the estates. Lord Newborough of the Glynllifon estate allowed the men to use Craig yr Undeb. Out of these meetings the North Wales Quarrymen's Union was created in 1874.

Keep following the old road to join the A4086 after passing through two more gates in quick succession. Turn right here and follow the path, part of Lôn Las Peris, to where it ends and carefully cross the road. Turn left along the track still part of Lôn Las Peris and pass through a short tunnel.

This track was part of the main line to Llanberis that closed in 1969.

Follow the track bed of the old railway line and continue to reach a barrier, there are white ringed marker posts, a part of the walk around Llyn Padarn.

Pass the barrier to arrive at toilets on the right. Turn left and down then almost immediately turn right. Follow the waymarked path into a rough car park then bear up to the access road. Turn left to the A4086.

Llyn Padarn is not particularly deep having a maximum depth of only 30 metres but is, however, the 6th deepest in Wales. Arctic Char, a species of fish dating back to the last Ice Age, is found here.

Turn left. Continue alongside the road to the Gwynedd County Council car park signed for the village. Cross the road at the crossing and continue up the street to Pete's Eats opposite Goodman Street.

Glynrhonwy Quarry pit to the right of the road

Walk 9

Moel Eilio via Bwlch y Groes

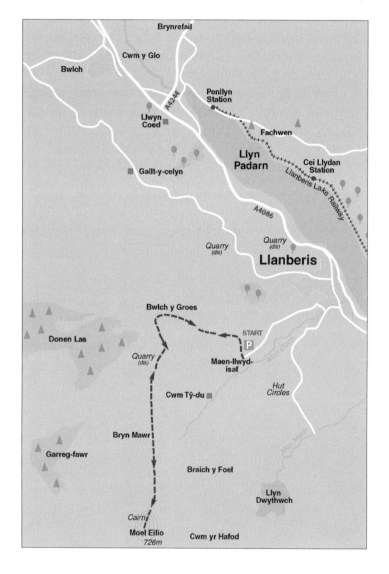

Walk details

Distance:	*4½ miles/7.2 kilometres*
Time (approx.):	*3¼ hours*
Map:	*OS Explorer 1:25,000 OL17 Snowdon/Yr Wyddfa*
Start:	*The car parking area at Maen-llwyd-isaf. Grid reference: SH 567594*
Access:	*From Llanberis turn up the road opposite The Heights – Ffordd Tŷ Du/Tŷ Du Road. Turn left 130 metres further. At the 'T' junction 160 metres up this turn right. Turn left 25 metres further again. Continue up the narrow road to where the tarmac ends by the ruins of Maen-llwyd-isaf*
Please note:	*There are very few passing places on the narrow road leading to the car park and the road has a gate. PLEASE close this*
	Moel Eilio is exposed to wind coming from the west
Going:	*On tracks or good clear paths*

Walk description

This is a gentle introduction to mountain walking. Navigation is easy as it follows a good track at the start to reach. Bwlch y Groes. From there a very prominent path is followed to reach a fence which leads directly to the summit. Views are superb and there is a fine circular stone shelter, a welcome wind break at times. Although the walk can be started in Llanberis the car parking area at Maen-llwyd-isaf avoids the road walking and, in my opinion, makes the walk more enjoyable.

Go up the track from the car parking area, with the ruin to the left, to a ladder stile and a gate. It is easier to pass through the gate! Follow either of the tracks ahead, they both join up ahead, and continue to another gate. Pass through this. A path goes off to the left immediately beyond. Ignore this. Continue along the track noting the spoil heaps of Glynrhonwy quarries over and down to the right.

These heaps are part of the upper workings that at one time were separate from the lower workings but later combined. Quarrying started in the mid-19th century. In 1882, when 90 men worked here, some 2,181 tons of slate were produced. The lower quarries were pioneers of internal rail systems. Work ceased and the quarries closed in 1939 when only 2 men worked there. This was just a little later than the lower ones which closed in the early 1930's. The lower quarries were used as bomb storage between 1940 and 1943 during World War II and subsequently for bomb disposal up to 1956. However, it was not until 1975 that the site was declared safe and free from explosives.

Keep following the track until 20 metres before the next gate and turn left up the obvious track. This becomes more of a wide path than a track. As height is gained there are great views.

Looking across to Deiniolen

Dinorwig Quarry is obvious cowering below the summit of Elidir Fawr 923 metres, Y Garn 947 metres, Glyder Fawr 1,001 metres and of course

60

Snowdon 1,085 metres. Over to the right is Cefn-du 442 metres, Anglesey and Yr Eifl in Llŷn.

Continue up on the wide path to reach a fence corner and ladder stile.

Looking down on Dinas

There is a great view of Anglesey and Caernarfon from here.

Ignore the stile but follow the fence up keeping it to the right to reach a redundant ladder stile. Pass through the gap to the left of it and, still following the path to the left of the fence, continue to a substantial stone shelter on the summit with views similar to the ones from the ladder stile at the fence corner.

Return to Maen-llwyd-isaf by retracing steps of the outward walk.

Elidir Fawr, Dinorwig slate quarry and Llanberis with Glyder Fawr on the right

Walk 10

'An alternative horseshoe', Moel Cynghorion, Foel Goch, Foel Gron and Moel Eilio

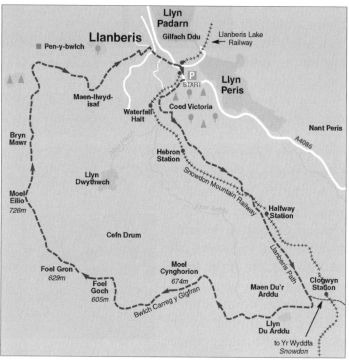

The start of the Llanberis Path

Walk details

Distance: 11 miles/17.6 kilometres

Time (approx.):   7 hours

Map: OS Explorer 1:25,000 OL17 Snowdon/Yr Wyddfa

Start: Snowdon Mountain Railway terminus

Access: Walk to the start from any of the car parks in
                     Llanberis

Please note: This is a long and tiring mountain day. The section
                     above Llyn Du'r Arddu after leaving the climber's
                     path to Clogwyn Du'r Arddu is not well defined and
                     care is needed to find the correct route for the
                     descent to the outflow of the lake. It is important to
                     find the line of cairns that lead on from here. Once
                     these have been left behind the route passes below a
                     steep grassy crag before going up to reach Bwlch
                     Cwm Brwynog

Going: On clearly followed roads, tracks or paths excepting
                     the section mentioned above where there are none

Walk description

This is a magnificent walk taking in the westerly
outliers of Snowdon. Although it is a long walk the
walking is generally easy other than occasional short
steeper sections and is easy to follow. Views are superb
especially of Clogwyn Du'r Arddu, perhaps the best
mountain rock climbing crag in Wales. Once the
hordes walking the Llanberis Path up Snowdon are left
behind it is quite possible that no-one else will be seen.

From the station walk up the road towards the
Royal Victoria Hotel to the roundabout some 150

metres away. Turn right and follow the road past a car park to a terrace of houses on the left, Vaynol Terrace dated 1906. Keep following the road as it becomes steep and passes the Pen y Ceunant tea rooms. The road continues up to take a sharp right hand turn around a building. The obvious start of the path is 200 metres further on to the left.

Follow this often busy path and after nearly 2 kilometres pass under the railway line. Continue to Halfway House where light refreshments can be purchased, although it is only open on in the summer. There is seating outside to rest aching limbs.

Joe Brown named one of his great climbs on Clogwyn Du'r Arddu after a girl who worked here in the early 1950's. She was called Vember. Fresh lemonade was traditionally sold here for weary walkers and climbers!

Continue gradually up. As height is gained there is a great view across to Clogwyn Du'r Arddu.

This is probably the finest rock climbing cliff in Wales and one of the most famous in Britain with many hard classic climbs. Rock climbers call it, affectionately, 'Cloggy'.

At the end of a fence on the right and where the

At the start of the 'climbers' path to Clogwyn Du'r Arddu with Allt Moses going up to the left

Llanberis Path bears up to the left a less clear path continues straight on from the final post on the fence. This is the start of the climber's path to Clogwyn Du'r Arddu. Follow this level path to some ruins on the left.

The view of Clogwyn Du'r Arddu and Llyn Du'r Arddu from here is spectacularly atmospheric. The massive mountain beyond the lake is Mynydd Mawr 698 metres.

Starting the 'climbers' path to Clogwyn Du'r Arddu from Allt Moses

Turn right at a pile of rocks on the right just beyond the ruins. Keeping to the high ground on the edge of the slope to the left a faint path is followed almost horizontally as it weaves between boulders.

Looking down from Moel Cynghorion to the Snowdon Ranger path

There are spectacular views of Clogwyn Du'r Arddu all along this section.

Continue slightly down to the top of the small moraine ridge above the small rocky valley below to the left with a stream flowing. When the path becomes steeper descend the moraine to the left to cross the stream.

Turn right to a cairn 50 metres away and the start of a cairned path. This quickly becomes clearer and crosses the slope. It becomes steeper as height is lost and passes below the toe of the broken grassy crag from where a short ascent leads to the ladder stile at Bwlch Cwm Brwynog

Climb over the stile at the fence and keeping to the left of it continue steeply up to reach and climb over another ladder stile. Keep following the fence to the summit area. There is a ladder stile over the fence to the very small cairn of quartz rocks marking the 674 metres high summit.

To the left of Snowdon 1,085 metres is Glyder Fawr 1,001 metres, Tryfan 917 metres, Y Garn 947 metres and Elidir Fawr 924 metres rising proudly above the huge Dinorwig slate quarry. To the right of Snowdon are Moel Hebog 783 metres, Moel yr Ogof 655 metres, Moel Lefn 638 metres and the Nantlle Ridge. To the right of that is Mynydd Mawr and closer to is Moel Eilio 726 metres. The huge cliff to the left of the Snowdon Ranger Path is Clogwyn Du'r Arddu which was seen earlier.

Keeping to the left of the fence follow it down to where it goes below some low cliffs. Stay high here and follow the ridge top path. The fence re-joins the path. Continue down to Bwlch Maesgwm.

Follow the steep path up to the summit of Foel Goch 605 metres. Climb over the ladder stile and again ignore the stile on the left. Keep the fence to the left and when that turns left carry straight on down to a col. Climb up to the subsidiary summit of Foel Gron.

There is a great view of Llanberis and Llyn Dwythwch down to the right.

Continue to the unmarked summit of Foel Gron, 629 metres, other than a fence post at the edge of the steep slope.

Climb over the ladder stile and keeping the fence

on the right descend slightly to Bwlch Cwm Cesig. Continue steeply up to climb a ladder stile over the wall. The summit of Moel Eilio is quickly reached where there is a fine circular stone shelter and a continuation of the fine views.

Looking down on Llyn Dwythwch

From the entrance to the shelter follow the fence on the left ignoring the ladder stile over it. Keep going down still keeping the fence to the left to a redundant ladder stile. Pass through the gap just to the right of it on the stony path. Keep going down on the stony path still with the fence on the left to the fence corner and ladder stile. The path /track is now less steep and continues down. At an obvious 'Y' junction much lower bear left and continue down to a track at Bwlch y Groes.

Turn right along this and follow it through 2 gates to reach the start of a narrow tarmac lane. Follow this down to a 'T' junction beyond the first houses. Turn right then left 25 metres further. Continue down to the next 'T' junction and turn right down to the High Street arriving opposite The Heights in the village.

Walk 11

Snowdon by the Llanberis Path

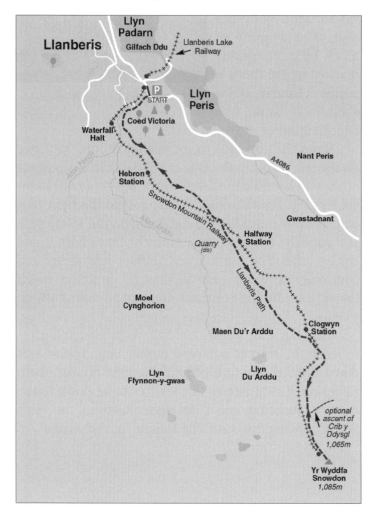

Walk details

Distance:	*9 miles/14.4 kilometres*
Time (approx.):	*6½ – 7 hours*
Map:	*OS Explorer 1:25,000 OL17 Snowdon/Yr Wyddfa*
Start:	*Snowdon Mountain Railway terminus, Llanberis*
Access:	*There are many car parks in Llanberis all of which are fee paying. From wherever cars are parked, make your way to the terminus of the railway*
Please note:	*This is a high mountain walk with some 975metres of ascent. The weather can change dramatically and very quickly. Even when it is hot and sunny in Llanberis it can be much colder on the summit. PLEASE dress accordingly and be prepared for a weather change. The ascent is the longest of all the routes up the mountain but it is the least steep! However, there are sections that are – the road at the start and Allt Moses to reach Clogwyn Station*
Going:	*On a minor road to start then a very obvious, wide trail often with many people all with the same thing on their mind – the summit of the highest mountain in Wales and England*

Before describing the walk a little bit of history and legend about the mountain.

A long time ago two kings of Britain, Nyniaw and Peibiaw became embroiled in a war. Rhita Gawr, the then King of Wales decided to put an end to it and killed both of them cutting off their beards in the process! When the other 28 Kings of Britain heard of this they decided to avenge them and war started again. Once more Rhita was victorious and cut off their beards too! A cloak was subsequently made from all these beards and it stretched from his shoulder to the floor – they must have been large beards. Rhita was known as a brave warrior and peace came about throughout the world. Unfortunately his demise came when he fought King Arthur as he wanted to add his beard to the cloak. Rhita was killed and it is said his tomb is under the pile of stones on the summit of Snowdon.

The first recorded ascent of Snowdon was made in 1639 by Thomas Johnson.

In 1838 Morris Williams became the first person to sell refreshments on the summit.

Walk description

This, the longest way up Snowdon is also the one with the more gradual gradient other than a couple of steeper sections. The views along the way are spectacular whilst the view from the summit is outstanding. Ireland is often seen on clear days. The only trouble is there will also be lots of other people enjoying the mountain too. It is also possible to include another mountain, Crib y Ddysgl, from Bwlch Glas either on the way up to the summit of Snowdon or on the way down. This gives a superb view of Snowdon and the Crib Goch ridge. Route finding in clear weather is not a problem but care is needed in misty conditions but finger stones at path junctions direct you to the correct way.

From the station walk up the road towards the Royal Victoria Hotel to the roundabout some 150 metres away. Turn right and follow the road past a car park to a terrace of houses on the left, Vaynol Terrace dated 1906. Keep following the road as it becomes steep and passes the Pen y Ceunant tea rooms. The road continues up to take a sharp right hand turn around a building. The obvious start of the path is 200 metres further on to the left.

Follow this often busy path and after nearly 2 kilometres pass under the railway line. Continue to Halfway House where light refreshments can be purchased, although it is only open in the summer. There is seating outside to rest aching limbs.

Joe Brown named one of his great climbs on Clogwyn Du'r Arddu after a girl who worked here in the early 1950's. She was called Vember. Fresh lemonade was traditionally sold for weary walkers and climbers!

Continue gradually up. As height is gained there is a great view across to Clogwyn Du'r Arddu.

This is probably the finest rock climbing cliff in Wales and one of the most famous in Britain with many hard classic climbs.

At the end of a fence on the right the path bears left and ascends quite steeply up what is known as Allt Moses to pass below the railway line close to Clogwyn Station. Just beyond there are great views of the Glyders and into Cwm Glas.

The upper part of it is known as Cwm Hetiau. In the days of open railway carriages hats of the ladies often blew away and ended up in the Cwm that became known as Cwm Hetiau. These hats were found by the locals and sold on! There are good views from here of the Glyders and Llanberis Pass.

Continue up now with the railway to the right to reach the finger stone on Bwlch Glas. This is also the junction of the PYG Track (the Miner's Track joins the PYG Track at the start of the zigzags).

An easy ascent of Crib y Ddysgl 1,065 metres can be

made from here by going up to the left on another obvious path.

Keep going up for a further 500 metres to the summit a few metres above Hafod Eryri and the Mountain Railway upper terminus. There is a circular plaque on top indicating all the surrounding features.

The descent reverses the outward walk which in clear weather is not a problem but be careful in mist to pick up the finger posts indicating the LLANBERIS PATH.

The 4.7 miles (7.5 kilometres) railway with a gauge of 2' 7 ½" (800mm) was opened on Easter Monday 1896. Colonel Sir Francis Marindin from the Board of Trade had previously inspected the line on the 27th March. Everything worked well and his only recommendation was that the wind speed be monitored and if too strong trains to be stopped. Carriages are always uphill of the locomotive and, as on that first run, not coupled to it. This was an important feature. On the descent that Easter Monday the engine, No 1 L.A.D.A.S., disengaged form the track and plunged over a cliff. Fortunately the driver and fireman were able to jump clear. The braking system on the carriages allowed them to safely come to a halt. Unfortunately two passengers seeing that the driver and fireman had leapt to safety also leapt from the train with one of them sustaining fatal injuries.

Because of this the line was closed for a year until flanged guard rails were installed each side of the rack rails. These keep the train engaged to the track if a carriage or locomotive starts to mount the running rails and gives constant traction throughout the whole journey.

Trains usually run from mid-March through October. Early and late in the season trains may not go all the way stopping at Clogwyn and bad weather may prevent trains

Snowdon summit at sunset

running at all. Trains are not time tabled but the first train leaves Llanberis at 09.00 and continues as long as there is demand. It takes about an hour for the train to reach the summit.

Walk 12

Vivian Quarry and Dinorwig Quarry Hospital

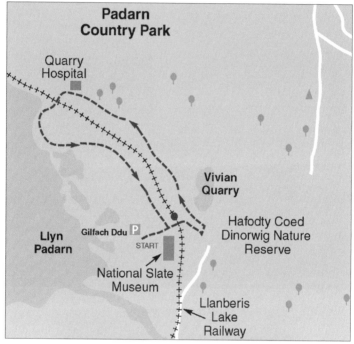

*Looking up at the Quarry Hospital from the terrace
below it*

Walk details

Distance: *1 mile/1.6 kilometres*

Time (approx.):   *45 minutes to 2 hours depending how long is spent at the hospital*

Map: *OS Explorer 1:25,000 OL17 Snowdon/Yr Wyddfa*

Start: *The Gwynedd County Council fee paying car park at Gilfach Ddu*

Access: *Directly from the car park*

Please note: *There are no particular hazards on this walk*

Going: *On roads and good tracks*

Walk description

This is a very pleasant and quite easy walk taking in the flooded pit of Vivian Quarry, part of the A1 incline and the Quarry Hospital. There is a great view of the surrounding mountains, Llanberis and Llyn Padarn from the hospital. This is well worth a visit. Inside is original gruesome medical equipment from the 1800's along with a ward, operating theatre an original X-Ray machine and a mortuary. The photographic exhibition depicts pictures of the quarrymen and memorabilia from local poet and dramatist T. Rowland Hughes. Opening times vary, but it is generally open 7 days a week from the end of May to early September. Check for other opening times.

Walk out of the car park towards the Llanberis Lake Railway. Cross the line and continue to the dive centre. Pass through the fine arch to the right into

Vivian Quarry. Follow the path to a viewing platform where divers below and climbers above may be seen.

Note the 'Blondin' dangling over the water.

Return through the arch and turn left up the side of the cleaned A1 incline. Where the 'cleaned' section ends turn left through the gap in the wall to a road. Turn left up this past viewpoint 1 where it is possible to look down into Vivian Quarry. Keep following the road and pass below the V2 incline noting the fine slate wall to the right. Continue up to the hospital.

There are fine views from here of Llanberis and mountains above it. These are right to left Moel Eilio 726 metres, Foel Gron 629 metres, Foel Goch 605 metres and Moel Cynghorion 674 metres. Snowdon 1,085 metres, is over to the left. Over to the right of Moel Eilio and much lower down the spoil heaps of Glynrhonwy Quarries are easily seen.

After visiting and admiring the fine view, descend the steps in front of the hospital to another lovely viewpoint. Follow the path down to a track and keeping left continue to the railway and the car park noting the fine V2 incline up to the left on the way.

A part of the gigantic Dinorwig Quarry work in Vivian Quarry ceased in 1958. It shared all the facilities of Dinorwig but was classed as separate from it. The water is around 18 metres (60 feet) deep.

The V2 incline was completed in 1873 and continued in service until the 1920's. The wagons had a level base and slates were loaded on to one of the wagons. The loaded wagon travelled down whilst the empty one went up. The incline was restored in 1998. The width of each track is 5'6" with both having a gradient of 1:1.3.

Blondins are specialised forms of Chain Inclines. They

allow loads to be picked up and transported and set down at any point along it.

Slate had many uses and apart from the obvious ones of slates for roofs and as building material it was used for the beds for snooker tables, cosmetics, building roads, walls, fences, homeopathic remedies, gravestones and cisterns. All the best snooker tables apparently have slate beds! Slate from the Llanberis quarries was exported worldwide.

The V2 incline

Walk 13

Short Walks from Gilfach Ddu

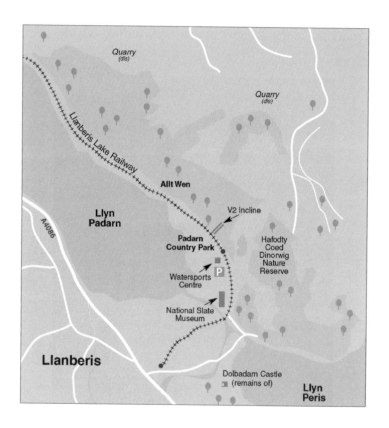

Walk details

Distance:	*None are longer than ½ mile*
Time (approx.):	*Each one of these walks can be walked in 30 minutes*
Map:	*OS Explorer 1:25,000 OL17 Snowdon/Yr Wyddfa*
Start:	*The Gwynedd County Council fee paying car park at Gilfach Ddu*
Access:	*Directly from the car park*
Please note:	*These walks are very easy and enjoyable and can be accomplished by wheelchair users*
Going:	*On good tracks or paths with very little, if any, ascent*

Walk description

The short trails here are steeped in history and with superb views, not only of the remains of the old quarry workings but also of Llyn Padarn, Llanberis and the mountains soaring above it.

Walk 1: Go out of the car park and cross the Llanberis Lake Railway line. Bear right and pass through the impressive slate bridge into Vivian Quarry.

Note the 'Blondin' cableway suspended above and the remarkable terracing, known as galleries, in the quarry.

Continue to a viewing platform. It is possible that divers will be here as well as rock climbers. Return under the bridge.

Walk 2: For this trail turn right after passing back

under the bridge, see the above walk, and follow the path to the right of the Llanberis Lake Railway buildings. Continue along the grass/gravel track to the foot of the very impressive V2 incline. Return to the level crossing and car park.

Vivian Quarry

Walk 3: At the far side of the car park opposite the entrance is a marker post and plaque to the right of it denoting the start of the Kingfisher Trail. Turn left and follow a compacted gravel/grass track. Turn right at the second turning, the first has tree roots sticking up. Go along to a viewing platform after crossing a bridge.

There is a good view of Llyn Padarn. The V2 incline is seen to the right as well as the Quarryman's Hospital. To the left the keep of Dolbadarn castle can be seen.

Return to where a two way arrow is seen on a circular plaque and bear left in front of it. Continue to a track. Turn left and follow the less wide track to the left of the main track to where it ends close to the pier. There are commanding views of Llyn Padarn and Llanberis from here. Return to the car park.

Dolbadarn castle was built in the early 1200's by Llywelyn ap Iowerth (otherwise known as Llywelyn the Great). It was a stamp of his authority of power in the area. Of simple design it pre-dates the fortifications of Edward I before he constructed his colonial castles. The impressive remnant of the keep stands over 15 metres high and was considered by the historian Richard Avent as 'the finest surviving example of a Welsh round tower'.

Llywelyn ap Iorwerth died in 1240. His grandson Llywelyn ap Gruffudd (or 'Llywelyn the Last Leader') gained control over Gwynedd by imprisoning his brother Owain Goch for over 20 years in the tower. After Llywelyn ap Gruffudd died his other brother Dafydd ap Gruffudd tried to maintain independence from English rule. Unfortunately Edward I captured the castle in 1283 and set about ruling Wales and building his castle in Caernarfon. Dolbadarn castle itself was plundered for its stone and wooden beams to help build the one in Caernarfon. Many artists have painted Dolbadarn castle, not least J. M. W. Turner (1775 – 1851) between 1798 and 1799.

The V2 incline was built in the 1860's and continued in service until the 1920's. The wagons had a level base and slates were loaded on to one of the wagons. The loaded wagon travelled down whilst the empty one went up. The incline was restored in 1998. The width of each track is 5'6" with both having a gradient of 1:1.3.

Blondins are specialised forms of Chain Inclines. They allow loads to be picked up and transported and set down at any point along it.

Slate had many uses and apart from the obvious ones of slates for roofs and as building material it was used for the beds for

Llyn Padarn and the Quarry Hospital

snooker tables, cosmetics, building roads, walls, fences, homeopathic remedies, gravestones and cisterns. All the best snooker tables apparently have slate beds! Slate from the Llanberis quarries was exported worldwide.

Llyn Padarn is not particularly deep having a maximum depth of only 100 feet. It is, however, the 6th deepest in Wales. It is home to the Arctic Char a species of fish dating back to the last Ice Age.

The Llanberis Lake Railway has a track gauge of 1'11½" along 2 miles of track along the shore of Llyn Padarn on part of the old track-bed of the slate railway to the harbour of Porth Dinorwig. This makes a very gentle journey alongside Llyn Padarn.

Although a dock existed at Porth Dinorwig a new one was built in 1828 after lime started to be extracted at Brynadda close by. Y Felinheli was the original name and the one used today.

Quarrying for slate started in Dinorwig in 1787 after a

The National Slate Museum

*Enjoying one of the trails by
Llyn Padarn*

lease had been granted by Assheton Smith whose family owned the Vaynol Estate. It became the second largest in the world only exceeded by its neighbour Penrhyn Quarry on the other side of the hill at Bethesda. At its peak the quarry produced over 100,000 tons per annum and employed 3,000 men. Production ceased in 1969.

Llanberis Lake Railway

Walk 14

Llyn Cwmffynnon

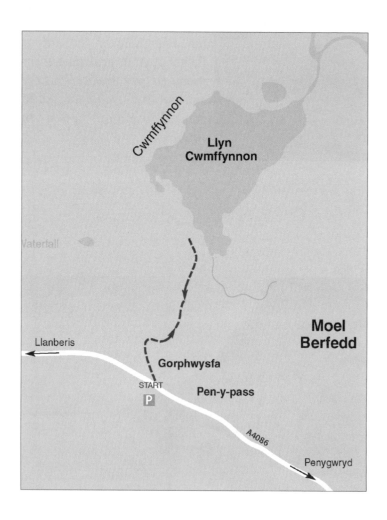

Walk details

Distance:	*¾ mile/1.2 kilometres*
Time (approx.):	*45 minutes walking time. This is a great picnicking spot and it is easy just to spend more time here anyway*
Map:	*OS Explorer 1:25,000 OL17 Snowdon/Yr Wyddfa*
Start:	*Snowdonia National Park Pen y Pass car park*
Access:	*Either park in the Pen y Pass car park if there is room, the park and ride bus from Nant Peris or catch the bus from Llanberis*
Please note:	*The car park at Pen y Pass is usually full by 08.00 in summer months and often in winter too. Although this is not a long walk it is situated in mountain terrain*
Going:	*On faint paths*

Walk description

The walk to this scenic lake has the feeling, once away from the bustle of Pen y Pass, of being remote yet it is only a very short distance away. This is lovely spot and well worth lingering here in the peaceful surroundings.

Walk out of the car park and cross the road to the Youth Hostel. Go through the gate immediately to the left of the building and walk up to a metal kissing gate 20 metres further. This leads to the open hillside. Bear left up the path and although quite steep it quickly reaches a storage tank with a metal grid over the top of it. There are some pretty bands of quartz here and a path junction. Go right here and follow the path to a

Snowdon and Crib Goch

Llyn Cwmffynnon and the slopes of Glyder Fach beyond

flat grassy hump overlooking the lake. Enjoy the surroundings and then return the same way to the car park.

There is a fine view of Snowdon 1,085 metres and the triangular form of Crib Goch 923 metres from here. The vast slopes of Glyder Fawr 1,001 metres and Glyder Fach 994 metres above the lake are impressive and a path up Glyder Fawr can just be discerned

The Snowdon Mountain Railway train nearing the summit

Walk 15

Around Nant Peris

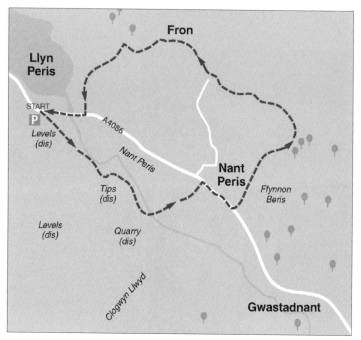

Nant Peris

Walk details

Distance:	*2 miles*
Time (approx.):	*1¼ hours*
Map:	*OS Explorer 1:25,000 OL17 Snowdon/Yr Wyddfa*
Start:	*At the car park, part of the old road, at grid reference SH 598587at the Nant Peris end of Llyn Peris*
Access:	*Follow the A4086 from Llanberis towards Nant Peris until the end of Llyn Peris is seen to the left. The car parking area is on a loop of old road to the right*
Please note:	*The section from Cae Gwyn to the final track has faint and, sometimes, confusing, paths. Care is needed to follow the correct way. There is also a steep drop into the stream beyond Fron but is avoidable by keeping high above it*
Going:	*The start of the walk follows a clear path to Cae Gwyn at the start and a good track towards the end. The paths between Cae Gwyn and the track leading to the main road are sometimes quite boggy in places*

Walk description

This is a pleasant walk starting off very gently along the valley floor. There are good views of Elidir Fawr and Glyder Fawr along here. When height is gained above Nant Peris the view towards the Crib Goch ridge is really good. There are good views of Nant Peris as well as a couple of pretty streams. Towards the end the Dinorwig Quarry spoil heaps are spectacular and are very much larger than imagined. When it is realised that for every ten tons quarried only around one ton was usable! All that waste is littered around the slopes of Elidir Fawr.

Pass through the obvious gate at the Nant Peris end of the car park and follow the track/path. Continue below old quarry workings.

These are the remnants of the Gallt y Llan quarry. A hillside working that started production around 1811. It was not a productive quarry. In fact only 90 tons of poor quality slate was produced in 1882 when three men were employed. There was a central incline servicing the terraces. Production ceased during the Second World War.

The huge bulk of Glyder Fawr 1,001 metres is seen ahead whilst to the left is Elidir Fawr 924 metres. In between is the rounded form of Y Garn 947 metres.

Keep following the path and after passing through a kissing gate the path rises slightly then descends to another kissing gate and gate close together before a fine footbridge. Cross this. Continue with a stream and

fence to the left past a gap to an old kissing gate at the slate fence and wall corner. Go through the gate and pass to the right of the children's play area. Pass to the right of the white house to go through a gate to reach the main road. The Vaynol Arms pub is on the right.

Cross the road and turn right. Follow the path by the side of the road to the sign for the Nant Peris park and ride.

Slate footbridge near end of walk

Turn left just beyond this in front of the sign for Cae Gwyn campsite. Follow the access road to this with small concrete pillars on the left at the start. Go straight ahead through a waymarked gate where the road bends left to the farmhouse. Walk gradually up the field with a wall then a fence to the left to climb over a ladder stile.

Continue straight ahead on a very faint path, which can be a little boggy in places, to reach a track. Cross over and continue to reach a grassy path. Follow this up through bracken. At the top of the short rise descend slightly to climb over a ladder stile before a footbridge. Cross this then up the steps at the far side and through another gate. Bear slightly right and up to the obvious old metal gate. Go through this to a track. Turn left and follow it down to a narrow tarmac lane.

Turn right and continue to the houses at Fron. Bear up to the right from the rough yard and through a gate. Bear slightly left and keeping the fence to the left continue to a gate through it. Go through the gate and veer slightly right until above a tumbling stream. Keeping above it continue down to a very narrow slate footbridge. Cross this, noting the lovely clear water, and climb over a dilapidated and fallen gate. Turn left and keeping the fence to the left continue down to a gate to the right of small compounds.

Go through the gate and bear right with the wall to the left. Go through a metal gate clad in chain link wire and continue down through another. Continue down to a track. Turn left down this to go through a gate to join a tarmac access lane. Follow this down and through the gate to the main road. Turn right back to the car park.

Walk 16

Coed Dinorwig and a brief look at Dinorwig Quarry

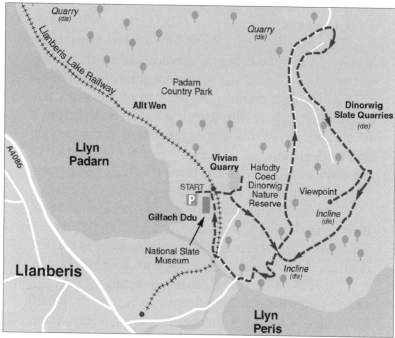

Llyn Padarn, Llanberis and Coed Dinorwig

Walk details

Distance: *2¾ miles/4.4 kilometres*

Time (approx.): *2 hours*

Map: *OS Explorer 1:25,000 OL17 Snowdon/Yr Wyddfa*

Start: *The Gwynedd County Council fee paying car park at Gilfach Ddu*

Access: *Directly from the car park*

Please note: *Do not enter any of the quarry remains*

Going: *On obvious paths, tracks or roads*

Walk description

This is a great walk taking in the flooded pit of Vivian Quarry part of the A1 incline and several drum houses. The walk from the upper one is through fine sessile oak woodland floored with bluebells in spring. The Anglesey Barracks are a stark reminder of how the quarrymen lived and worked. There is a great view of the surrounding mountains, Llanberis and Llyn Padarn from the top of the incline before going into the woodland although the one from the viewpoint later in the walk is better.

View from the start of the walled path – Llyn Peris, Dolbadarn castle and Moel Eilio rising above Llanberis

93

Walk out of the car park towards the Llanberis Lake Railway. Cross the line and continue to the dive centre. Pass through the fine arch to the right into Vivian Quarry. Follow the path to a viewing platform where divers below and climbers above may be seen.

Note the 'Blondin' cableway suspended above and the remarkable terracing, known as galleries, in the quarry.

Return through the arch and turn left up the side of the A1 incline to where the cleaned section ends. Continue up the 'uncleaned section' to the drum house seen at the top where there is a fine example of the braking mechanism as well as the drum. Keep following the incline steeply up to another but much more ruinous one. Continue below the drum of this and the footbridge. Turn left immediately beyond the bridge and go up to a marker post.

Turn right. Follow the path up through very fine sessile oak woodland, a part of Coed Dinorwig and the Nature Reserve.

Bluebells carpet the ground in spring.

Continue up to where a path goes off to the right. Turn right here to view the Anglesey Barracks. Return to the path and continue up steeply to reach a level track going off to the right. Turn right along this, ignoring the path going up to the left, and follow it up to a terrace of small cottages. Just past these the track becomes a tarmacked road. Continue along this to a large looping layby on the right. In the right hand corner close to the bus stop is a kissing gate. Pass through this and follow the track going slightly up at the start, then along to the fine ruin of the mill. Turn right at the end of this and continue to a wonderful view point.

The mountains forming the skyline are left to right,

Starting the walled path looking out to Llanberis and Llyn Padarn

Crib y Ddysgl 1,065 metres at the end of Crib Goch ridge and close to the summit of Snowdon which it hides. To the right is Moel Cynghorion 674 metres, Foel Goch 605 metres, Foel Gron 629 metres and Moel Eilio 726 metres.

Assheton-Smith the landowner started slate quarrying here in 1782. By the turn of the century there were 13 levels some 18 – 23 metres high. The first incline was built in 1789 but sledges were more often used until 1816.One of the features of Dinorwig Quarry was that there were 2 main inclines. These had many sections or pitches. Each pitch would connect 2 or perhaps 3 terraces. Steam locomotives arrived in the 1870's with petrol ones arriving in 1930. There was perhaps 50 miles of railway lines and 15 miles of compressed air pipes. The main mill was on a level with Dinorwig village and is best seen when walking back from the viewpoint. 'Blondins' were installed in the 1930's and electric power came from Cwm Dyli in 1905. The quarry's output in the late 1890's was 100,000 tons per annum. When you think that would have produced a million tons of waste to be scattered over the slopes of Elidir Fawr! Almost 3,000 workers were employed at that time. Work stopped in 1969.

Return to the end of the mill to a kissing gate on the right with a path bending to the right. Ignore the kissing gate straight ahead with a track continuing straight ahead. The path bears right and continues down the straight incline with a fence to the left and passes between high slate walls.

Note the frequent holes in the slate that housed the holding brackets for the incline rails as well as lengths of the 'I' section line, the rollers and occasional lengths of wire.

Pass between more walls to where the path levels and reaches a drum house. Bear right and step through a low wall and pass to the right of house. Turn left and keep following the fence down passing several blue ringed marker posts to where it is possible to turn right through a wide doorway to view Anglesey Barracks. This time from a different angle!

Return to the path and continue down the incline to where it levels and bears right. Carry on until below an ancient metal footbridge with a ruined drum house just beyond it. These were seen on the outward walk. Go up to the right immediately before going underneath the bridge to a clear path. Turn left across the bridge to a remarkable walled path. Follow this down to where it leaves it to descend a steep slope interspersed with irregular slate steps and a final short section of walled path to reach the road. Turn right to the roundabout then right again to follow the footpath to the right of the slate museum and left of the Llanberis Railway track back to the car park.

Walk 17

The ascent of Cefn Du

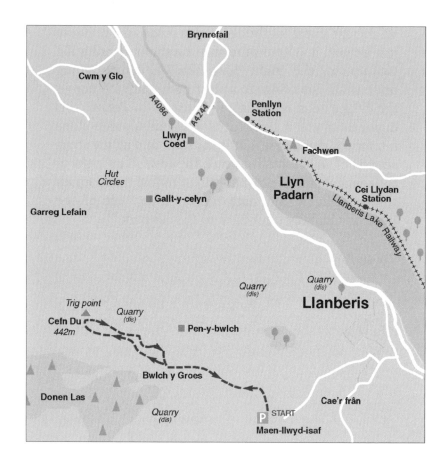

Walk details

Distance:	*3 miles/4.8 kilometres*
Time (approx.):	*2 hours*
Map:	*OS Explorer 1:25,000 OL17 Snowdon/Yr Wyddfa*
Start:	*The car parking area at Maen-llwyd-isaf.* *Grid reference: SH 567594*
Access:	*From Llanberis turn up the road opposite The Heights, Ffordd Tŷ Du/Tŷ Du Road. Turn left 130 metres further. At the 'T' junction 160 metres further turn right then left 25 metres further again. Continue up the narrow road to where the tarmac ends by the ruins of Maen-llwyd-isaf*
Please note:	*DO NOT enter any of the workings or venture onto the spoil heaps. There is much loose rock*
Going:	*On good tracks or paths*

Walk description

Although this walk can be started from Llanberis the car parking area at Maen-llwyd-isaf avoids the road walking and, in my opinion, makes the walk more enjoyable. It is a good walk visiting a fine windswept summit. It is easy to follow and makes a great afternoon excursion. There are some great views and much historical interest.

Go up the track from the car parking area, with the ruin to the left, to a ladder stile and a gate. It is easier to pass through the gate! Follow either of the tracks ahead, they both join up ahead, and continue to another gate. Pass through this. A path goes off to the left immediately beyond. Ignore this and continue along the track noting the spoil heaps of Glyrhonwy quarries.

These heaps are part of the upper workings that at one time were separate from the lower workings but later combined. Quarrying started in the mid-19th century. In 1882, when 90 men worked here, some 2,181 tons of slate were produced. The lower quarries were pioneers of internal rail systems. Work ceased and the quarries closed in 1939 when only 2 men worked there. This was just a little later than the lower ones which closed in the early 1930's. The lower quarries were used as bomb storage between 1940 and 1943 during World War II and subsequently for bomb disposal up to 1956. However, it was not until 1975 that the site was declared safe and free from explosives.

Looking towards Cefn-du

Keep following the track to the next gate. Pass through this and turn immediately right. Follow the track up with wall and fence to the right to a gate on the right at the junction with a track coming in from the left. Turn left along it then right 20 metres further up the rough track. Continue up this to where the fence on the left kinks leftwards and passes above the quarry on the left, Chwarel Fawr part of the Cefn-du workings.

Cefn Du slate quarry opened in the 18th century and was a going concern until it closed in 1928. In 1882 production peaked at 5,640 tons when it employed 197 men. The spoil heaps make for a spectacular feature.

Turn right onto the narrow grassy path. Follow it up becoming more obvious as height is gained to reach the trig point at 441 metres and the summit of the hill at 442 metres a few metres away sporting a ruin. This is part of the old radio station situated directly below in Ceunant.

An old building in this tiny village, just outside Waunfawr, was at one time at the forefront of wireless technology and commissioned by the Marconi Wireless and Telegraphy Company in 1914.It also housed the Beacon Climbing Centre, until it too moved. It was from here that the first radio transmission from the UK to Australia was made on the 22nd September 1918. Technology kept on being improved and the first pictures were transmitted to the USA in 1932. Unfortunately much newer technology forced closure in 1938. It was deemed to be the most important such station in Britain. Not only did it handle imperial communications it dealt with international ones as well. The receiving station was at Tywyn (nprn421024). After closure it had the dubious distinction of being a strip club in the 1970's!

There are great views from the summit, Eliir Fawr 924 metres, Y Garn 947 metres, Glyder Fawr 1,001 metres, Snowdon 1,085 metres and Moel Eilio 726 metres close to and just opposite here. To the right is Mynydd Mawr 698 metres and right again the geologically interesting rocks on top of Moel Tryfan 427 metres. Right again Yr Eifl is seen as well as a superb vista over Anglesey and down to Caernarfon.

Follow the left hand branch of the 'Y' junction. Ignore the right hand path as this was the path of the ascent. Follow the narrow grassy path that very quickly becomes much more obvious to reach a fence and wall. Keeping these to the left continue down with a very impressive view in front to join a prominent track. Turn right down this and follow it keeping the fence to the left. Pass to the left of ruins and where Llanberis and Llyn Padarn come into view.

Bear right and continue down keeping the wall and

Deiniolen from the descent path

fence to the left to the gate on the left reached earlier. Continue down to the gate and the track leading down to Maen-llwyd-isaf. Follow it back as for the outward walk to the car parking area.

Walk 18

Llyn Padarn View

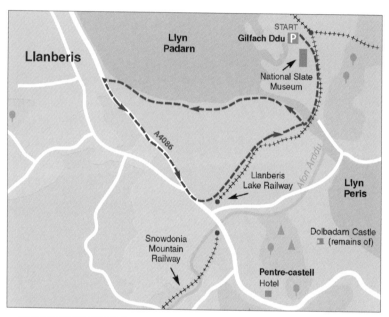

The Quarry Hospital above Llyn Padarn

Walk details

Distance:	*1½ miles*
Time (approx.):	*Allow an hour*
Map:	*OS Explorer 1:25,000 OL17 Snowdon/Yr Wyddfa*
Start:	*The Gwynedd County Council fee paying car park at Gilfach Ddu*
Access:	*Directly from the car park*
Please note:	*This is another walk that can be completed by the less abled*
Going:	*On a good track, path and a wide roadside pavement*

Walk description

This trail is great little stroll giving an excellent view of Llyn Padarn. It also crosses, reputedly, the shortest river in Britain. Views are lovely of the mountains soaring up behind Llanberis and also towards Dolbadarn castle.

Walk out of the car park to the railway line and turn right on the path by the side of the road with the railway to the left, Continue to where the wall bounding the museum bears right. Follow the wall round to the footbridge spanning the river, reputedly the shortest in Britain! Cross the bridge and through the gate. Turn right immediately on a path by the side of the river to reach the lake and follow its margin around to a kissing gate. Or, follow the white ringed marker posts to this point which is better for wheelchair users.

Dolbadarn castle and the Llechog Ridge

Dolbadarn castle over to the left can be seen rising above the trees.

The castle was built in the early 1200's by Llywelyn ap Iorwerth (otherwise known as Llywelyn the Great). It was a stamp of his authority of power in the area. Of simple design it pre-dates the fortifications of Edward I before constructed his 'Ring of Iron' castles. The impressive remnant of the keep stands over 15 metres high and was considered by the historian Richard Avent as 'the finest surviving example of a Welsh round tower'.

Llywelyn ap Iorwerth died in 1240. His grandson Iorwerth ap Gruffudd (or Iorwerth the Last') gained control over Gwynedd by imprisoning his brother Owain Goch for over 20 years in the tower. After Iorwerth ap Gruffudd died his other brother Dafydd ap Gruffudd tried to gain independence from English rule. Unfortunately Edward I captured the castle in 1283 and set about ruling Wales and building his castle in Caernarfon. Dolbadarn castle itself was plundered for its stone and wooden beams to help build the one in Caernarfon. Many artists have painted Dolbadarn castle, not least J. M. W. Turner (1775 – 1851) between 1798 and 1799.

Pass through the gate and follow the path straight ahead to reach a footbridge. A hump needs care for wheelchair users. Cross the bridge into a car park. Bear right past an information panel and past the children's play area to reach the road. Turn left and follow the path alongside this. Go past the car park entrance and the Electric Mountain building. Continue to the Llanberis Lake Railway station. Turn left through a gate and follow the path to the left of the railway line to the footbridge crossed earlier. Return to the car park as for the outward walk.

Llyn Padarn is not particularly deep having a maximum depth of only 30 metres but is, however, the 6th deepest in Wales. Arctic Char, a species of fish dating back to the last Ice Age, is found here.

The Llanberis Lake Railway has a track gauge of 1'11½" along 2 miles of track along the shore of Llyn Padarn on part of the old track-bed of the slate railway to Porth Dinorwig. This makes a very gentle and reccommended journey alongside Llyn Padarn.

Although a dock existed at Porth Dinorwig a new one was built in 1828 after lime started to be extracted at Brynadda close by. Port Dinorwic has been re-named Y Felinheli.

Quarrying for slate started in Dinorwig in 1787 after a lease had been granted by Assheton Smith whose family owned the Vaynol Estate. It became the second largest in the world only exceeded by its neighbour Penrhyn Quarry on the other side of the hill at Bethesda. At its peak the quarry produced over 100,000 tons per annum and employed 3,000 men. Production ceased in 1969.

Slate had many uses and apart from the obvious ones of slates for roofs and as building material it was used for the beds for snooker tables, cosmetics, building roads, walls, fences, homeopathic remedies, gravestones and cisterns. All the best snooker tables apparently have slate beds! Slate from the Llanberis quarries was exported worldwide.

Walk 19

Cei Llydan to Gilfach Ddu

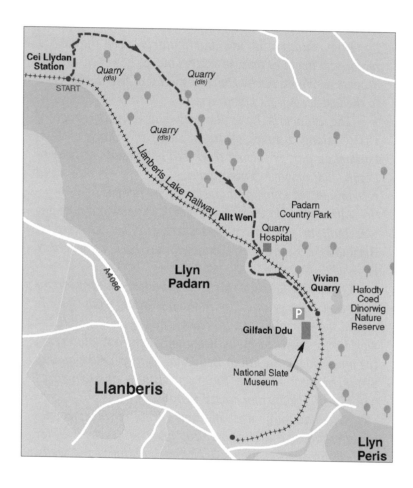

Walk details

Distance:	*2 miles/3.2 kilometres*
Time (approx.):	*1¼ hours and if visiting the Quarry Hospital add an extra hour*
Map:	*OS Explorer 1:25,000 OL17 Snowdon/Yr Wyddfa*
Start:	*Cei Llydan station*
Access:	*Directly from the station*
Please note:	*Steep to start and some muddy sections in wet weather. When buying a ticket for the train ask for a reduction in the ticket cost because you are walking back from Cei Llydan. The train journey is best started from Gilfach Ddu. Cars therefore need to be left at the Gwynedd County Council fee paying car park there. Trains operate from late February to early November*
Going:	*Easily followed paths and tracks*

Walk description

This pleasant walk has some fine woodland much of it with sessile oaks. These have contorted branches and create an air of magic. Starting off with a gentle train ride the start of the walk is from the woodland station of Cei Llydan. There is also a picnic site across the line on the shore of Llyn Padarn.

'Alice' at Cei Llydan station

From the platform turn left at the finger post signed for the woodland trails. Bear right and go up past ruins. Go up to the left at the path junction to a twin footbridge. Go left and up to a wood open sided information shelter. Again go left as indicated. At the grassy glade go left once more and follow the zigzagging path up to a cottage. Go up steps to the right to reach a track. Turn right along this.

There is a good view of Moel Cynghorion 674 metres and Llanberis along here.

Pass below a bridge and ignore the path going down to the right immediately beyond this. Keep following the track ignoring all turnings. Go past the turning signed for Coed Mabon. The track descends, after a no vehicles beyond this point sign, to the very pretty Nant Fachwen. There is a predominance of sessile oak trees here.

Go across the slate bridge and bear right to go through a gate. Go up to the left at the path junction here and climb gradually up. In wet weather this is slippery. At the path junction with a path coming up from the right keep going up to where the path levels at a small clearing and vantage point.

There is a magnificent view from here of Snowdon 1,085 metres and left to right, Moel Cynghorion, Foel Goch 605 metres, Foel Gron 629 metres and Moel Eilio 726 metres rising directly above Llanberis.

The path now starts to descend and reaches a 'Y' junction by point 4! Go right and down below ruins. Keep descending to a level section which leads to the Quarry Hospital after passing the mortuary dated 1906! The hospital is well worth a visit when open. There are also great views from here. Go down the steps in front of the hospital to a grassy area overlooking Llyn Padarn. Follow the path around and down to a path junction at a multi-coloured marker post. Either go straight ahead to the station or follow the marker posts to the car park.

The Llanberis Lake Railway utilises the track bed of the old Padarn Railway, a 4' (1,219mm) gauge line connecting the quarries to Y Felinheli (Porth Dinorwig). This closed in October 1961 and the rails lifted between 16th May 1962 and February 1963. In July 1966 Lowry Porter from Southend on Sea proposed building a railway running from Gilfach Ddu along the 3 miles long eastern side of Llyn Padarn. In 1969 Dinorwig Quarry closed at short notice. Gwynedd County Council bought the track bed of the Padarn Railway in June 1970 agreeing for it to be used for the lake railway project.

The new railway was built to a gauge of 1' 11½" (597 mm) although the quarries used a most unusual gauge of 1' 10¾" (578 mm). This was unfortunate because all the rolling stock had to be altered to suit the new gauge. The track continued to be laid throughout 1970 and on 28th May 1971 the railway officially opened. However, because the carriages had to be redesigned the first public trains did not run until 19th July 1971, just in time for the school holidays! By the end of that first season over 30,00 passengers had been carried. The extension into Llanberis was opened in June 2003.

Walk 20

Coed Doctor and Llyn Tomos Lewis

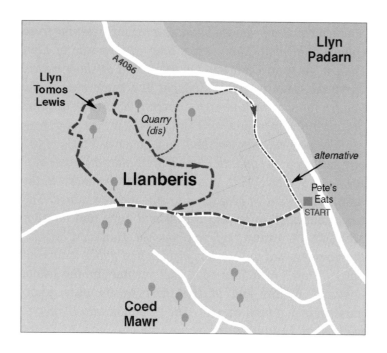

Walk details

Distance: 1 *mile*

Time (approx.):   *Allow 45 minutes*

Map: *OS Explorer 1:25,000 OL17 Snowdon/Yr Wyddfa*

Start: *Goodman Street, Llanberis. This is opposite Pete's Eats*

Access: *From any of the car parks in the village*

Please note: *Several alternatives are possible. A main walk is described and one alternative*

Going: *On good gravel paths*

Walk description

This is a very pleasant walk in some wonderful woodland. It is a gem, especially so with being situated in the middle of the village! There are signs of slate quarrying in several places. The name of the quarry is Twll Tomos Lewis part of the Goodman's Quarry workings. Many of the trees are sessile oaks. These have wonderful contorted branches. There are also birch, alder (these love damp ground) and willow (these also love wet areas). Many water birds can be seen on Llyn Tomos Lewis and include moorhen, coots, mallards and tufted ducks. The lake is a remnant of the old slate workings. Some of the woodland birds seen here are little owls, buzzards, woodpeckers and tree creepers. There are also bats with, apparently, 6 species having been seen in one night! Mammals such as badgers, stoats and weasels are often seen. Reptiles can be found in the drier areas and these include adders, common lizards and slow worms. Frogs love the place!

The old quarry was developed in the 1870's and 80's and only produced a few hundred tons per annum and closed in 1890. For such a small undertaking it was connected by its own tramway to Llanberis station.

Walk up Goodman Street ignoring all turnings to left and right. Continue past Cambrian Terrace with Warren Street to the right. Keep going up the road to where Lôn Clegir starts by the speed de-restriction signs, Ignore the kissing gate on the left and continue another 25 metres to an information panel and kissing gate on the right. Pass through the gate and follow the obvious gravel path. When this starts to descend there is a circle of wood seats made from tree branches and trunks.

Llyn Tomos Lewis

Continue down the good path to where a path goes off to the right at a junction. Ignore this and continue down. Continue across a footbridge to reach a fenced off quarry. Follow the path left and go around it going down the left hand side of it. Keep following the main path down steps to the point where Llyn Tomos Lewis can be seen through the trees to the right. Continue over the stream to a gate. Pass through this. Turn right along the fenced path with the caravan site to the left to a footbridge over the outflow of the lake.

Cross the bridge and turn right and follow the path to go through a kissing gate. Follow the main path up to the remains of a reservoir dam. Turn left over this. At the next path junction turn right. Go up to the next junction and turn left. Keep going up and pass a small long abandoned small quarry. Climb up a short flight of steps and then down a similar number. Continue to a crossroads of paths. An alternative finish starts here and is only one of several that are possible. This is described below whilst the others are left to your imagination! Go straight across up a short flight of steps and continue to a gate. Pass through this, with sheds to the left, and continue to a road – Warren Street. Turn right and then left 25 metres ahead down Goodman Street back to the start.

One alternative of several here, although not as good as the main walk, is to turn left and down at the cross roads. Go along to a long flight of steps. Descend these to a path junction. Turn right and continue to and across a section of duckboards to go through a gate to the road that passes through the village. Follow this back to the start of the walk.

Walk 21

Coed Mawr

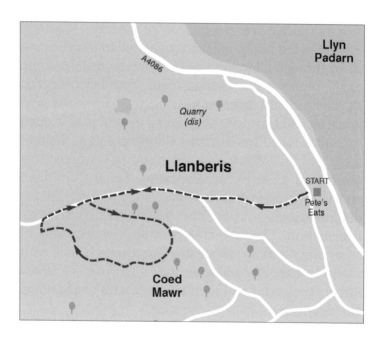

Walk details

Distance: *1½ miles*

Time (approx.):   *Allow an hour*

Map: *OS Explorer 1:25,000 OL17 Snowdon/Yr Wyddfa*

Start: *Goodman Street, Llanberis. This is opposite Pete's Eats*

Access: *From any of the car parks in the village*

Going: *Road, track or paths*

Walk description

Although short this is a very pleasant walk with some great views.

Walk up Goodman Street which is initially quite steep and ignoring all turnings to where it levels. Go past the gate and information panel for the Coed Doctor walk (walk 20). Continue up the road past an emergency exit for the works on the right and past Ael y Bryn the house on the left to a finger post on the left immediately beyond a wriggly tin garage. Go through the old sheet metal kissing gate and follow the path to the left with a wall on the left. Pass above the house and continue to where the path widens to a track and goes up to a kissing gate.

Pass through this to houses on the left. On the right at the start of a tarmac road is a finger post and track going up to the right with a sign for Coed Mawr on the gate. Follow this track up to a house. Pass right of this to a low marker post with a choice of directions.

There is great view of Dinas ahead. This is the hill with an Iron Age fort on top visited on walk 4. Moel Eilio 726 metres, is the mountain to the left of Dinas and further left again is Moel Cynghorion 674 metres and Snowdon 1,085 metres is visible over to the left of that.

Bear right and through the right hand gap of three possibilities. This has a high wall end each side of it. Continue past a low wall end and bear right to cross a ladder stile.

Over to the right the Glynrhonwy slate quarry is easily seen. Looking back Elidir Fawr 924 metres, Y Garn 947 metres and Glyder Fawr 1,001 metres are clearly visible.

The path goes right and descends and crosses a small stone lined ditch from where a short easy ascent leads up to a large 'spreading' oak tree. Descend the path and keep above a ruin down to the right.

This is all that remains of the early 17th century house built by the Dean of Westminster, Dr Goodman. Later he bequeathed it in order to help establish Christ's Hospital in Ruthin.

Continue down to a kissing gate on the right. Go through this to the narrow road. Turn right along it back to the start of the walk. Or, for a longer walk only go as far as the entrance to Coed Doctor and turn left into it. Follow the directions as for walk 20 back to the start. This is a good combination.

Pete's Eats, Llanberis

Walk 22

Llanberis, Cwm y Glo, Fachwen and back to Llanberis Circular Walk

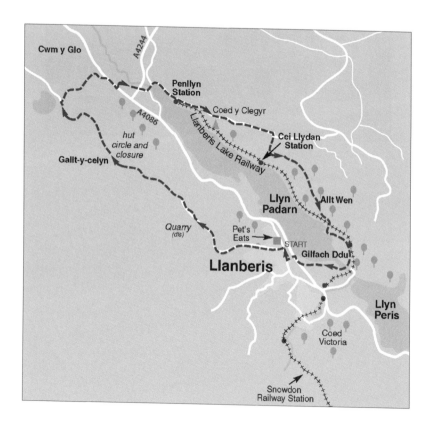

Walk details

Distance:	*6¾ miles*
Time (approx.):	*4½ hours*
Map:	*OS Explorer 1:25,000 OL17 Snowdon/Yr Wyddfa*
Start:	*Goodman Street, Llanberis. This is opposite Pete's Eats*
Access:	*From any of the car parks in the village*
Please note:	*Take care when crossing the two busy roads*
Going:	*Road, track or paths*

Walk description

This is a wonderful higher level version for a walk around Llyn Padarn combining, what I think, are the better sections of walks 1 and 8. Views are superb from the high point on the road although there are great views throughout. There are some longish sections of uphill but these are road based although one close to the end is somewhat steep as it passes through some fine woodland.

Walk up Goodman Street which is initially quite steep. Ignoring all turnings continue to where the road levels. Keep following the road and pass a ruin seen to the left of the road.

This is all that remains of the early 17th century house built by the Dean of Westminster, Dr Goodman. Later he bequeathed it in order to help establish Christ's Hospital in Ruthin.

Continue along the pretty road to the spoil heaps

of Glynrhonwy slate quarry. The road rises and passes between two very impressive pits. The pit on the left has some pinnacles whilst the one on the right has a deep looking black pool.

The Glynrhonwy quarries closed in 1930. Between 1940 and 1943 during the Second World War they were requisitioned by the Air Ministry to store over 18,000 tons of bombs and explosives. Subsequently the quarries were used for bomb disposal. This continued up to 1956. However, it was not until 1975 that the site was cleared and declared safe and free from explosives. The left hand quarry was used as a venue by Ron Howard for the film 'Willow' starring Val Kilmer in 1968.

Developed in the 1870's the site incorporated several small scratchings. There was a large mill and a rail system on several levels. The quarry was one of the pioneers installing internal rail systems. It was the largest undertaking on the eastern side of the valley. In 1883 some 1,789 tons were produced when 70 men were employed. Later output increased to around 40 tons per man per year.

Looking back from here Snowdon 1,085 metres can be seen.

The road undulates, but generally rises, to reach the high point.

Just before reaching this on the right and just below a lone and large hawthorn small stone rings can be seen. These are the remains of Iron Age round huts that were sited here some 2,000 years ago.

The view from the high point is very good. Anglesey is spread out with Holyhead Mountain 220 metres on the far horizon. Puffin Island to the right is also prominent. Llyn Padarn covers the valley floor with the cluster of houses above it, Deiniolen, looking like an Andalusian village. To the right is Elidir Fawr 924 metres, Y Garn 947 metres and

Glyder Fawr 1,001 metres. The gash of Llanberis Pass with the road snaking up it, splits these mountains to those on the right. These are the pinnacles of Crib Goch, Crib y Ddysgl 1,065 metres and finally the pyramidal shaped summit of Snowdon 1,085 metres.

The road now descends quite steeply and a tree lined reservoir is seen ahead. When the road levels there is a finger post on the right at the junction of a good track signed for Lôn Bwlch. Turn right down this and follow the track as it passes between houses and descends to a finger post and steps on the right where the track swings 90 degrees to the left. Turn right down the steps. Descend the path with a tiny stream on the left to where the path becomes enclosed and continues to reach a narrow road. Walk down this to the road through the village. Turn right to reach the A4086. Turn right along the roadside path to where it ends. On the small cliff face to the right is a plaque commemorating an accident hereabouts.

One of the most dreadful accidents to happen in the area occurred on Wednesday 30th June 1869. It was a very hot day. Two carts carrying nitro-glycerine, to be used in the Glynrhonwy quarries, exploded. Five people and two horses were killed instantly. Another 8 were seriously injured with one of them dying a few days later. The explosion was so fierce that it created two craters 10 feet deep and 30 feet wide! Not a house within a mile radius was left unscathed. No trace of was found of either the horses or two of the men. Some human remains were found a mile away and a wheel from one of the carts was found on the road close to the summit of the road previously walked!

Cross the road, carefully, onto the path at the far side and turn right along it to the sign for Y Fricsan. Turn left and walk up to a 'T' junction. Y Fricsan is up to the left. Turn right and follow the path to another main road the A4244. Cross this carefully and walk straight ahead down to the end of a pretty bridge at the end of Llyn Padarn. Turn left over it.

The view up Llyn Padarn from the bridge is superb. On the left of the lake is Elidir Fawr 924 metres whilst Snowdon is to the right of it.

At the far end of the bridge on the right is a plaque with a lovely poem written by Gillian Clarke.

But for how?
Cherish these mountains, born in fire and ash
out of the sea to make this wilderness,
asleep for aeons beneath ice and snow,
carved by the shifting glaciers long ago,
till ten millennia back, the last ice age
made right for fern and purple saxifrage
this place whose evolution's given birth
to the rare Snowdon Lily's home on earth
but all could go with the melting snow

Turn right where the road is signed for Fachwen and follow this road up through woodland to a phone box, with no phone, on the left. White markers have been followed from the bridge and these are followed for the rest of the walk. Continue past this to a gate on the right. Pass through this and descend the path to an access track. Turn right down this and follow it past houses and a turning to Coed Mabon. The track descends, after a no vehicles sign, to the very pretty Nant Fachwen. There is a predominance of sessile oak trees here.

Go across the slate bridge and bear right to go through a gate. Go up to the left at the path junction here and climb gradually up. In wet weather this is slippery. At the path junction with a path coming up from the right keep going up to where the path levels at a small clearing and vantage point.

There is a magnificent view from here of Snowdon 1,085 metres and left to right, Moel Cynghorion, Foel Goch 605 metres, Foel Gron 629 metres and Moel Eilio 726 metres rising directly above Llanberis.

The path now starts to descend and reaches a 'Y' junction by point 4! Go right and down below ruins. Keep descending to a level section which leads to the Quarry Hospital after passing the mortuary dated 1906! The hospital is well worth a visit when open. There are also great views from here. Go down the steps in front of the hospital to a grassy area overlooking Llyn Padarn. Follow the path around and down to a path junction at a multi-coloured marker post. Either go straight ahead to the station or follow the marker posts to the car park in Gilfach Ddu and the Llanberis Lake Railway.

The Llanberis Lake Railway utilises the track bed of the old Padarn Railway, a 4' (1,219mm) gauge line connecting the quarries to Y Felinheli (Porth Dinorwig). This closed in October 1961 with the line being lifted between 16th May 1962 and February 1963. In July 1966 A. Lowry Porter from Southend on Sea proposed building a railway running from Gilfach Ddu along the 3 miles long eastern side of Llyn Padarn. In 1969 Dinorwig Quarry closed at short notice. Gwynedd County Council bought the track bed of the Padarn Railway in June 1970 agreeing for it to be used for the lake railway project.

The new railway was built to a gauge of 1' 11½" (597 mm) although the quarries used a most unusual gauge of 1' 10¾" (578 mm). This was unfortunate because all the rolling stock had to be altered to suit the new gauge. The track continued to be laid throughout 1970 and on 28th May 1971 the railway officially opened. However, because the carriage shad to be redesigned the first public trains did not run until 19th July 1971, just in time for the school holidays! By the end of that first season over 30,00 passengers had been carried. The extension into Llanberis was opened in June 2003.

Continue through the car park and follow the path alongside the road and railway with the National Slate Museum on the right. Continue to where the wall bounding the museum bears right. Follow the wall round to the footbridge spanning the river, reputedly the shortest in Britain! Cross the bridge and through the gate. Turn right immediately on a path by the side of the river to reach the lake and follow its margin around to a kissing gate. Or, follow the white ringed marker posts to this point.

Dolbadarn castle was built in the early 1200's by Llywelyn ap Iowerth (otherwise known as Llywelyn the Great). It was a stamp of his authority of power in the area. Of simple design it pre-dates the fortifications of Edward I before he constructed his 'Ring of Iron' castles. The impressive remnant of the keep stands over 15 metres high and was considered by the historian Richard Avent as 'the finest surviving example of a Welsh round tower'.

Llywelyn ap Iorwerth died in 1240. His grandson Llywelyn ap Gruffudd (or 'Llywelyn the Last Leader') gained control over Gwynedd by imprisoning his brother Owain Goch for over 20 years in the tower. After Llywelyn ap Gruffudd died his other brother Dafydd ap Gruffudd tried to maintain independence from English rule. Unfortunately Edward I captured the castle in 1283 and set about ruling Wales and building his castle in Caernarfon.

Dolbadarn castle was plundered for its stone and wooden beams to help build the one in Caernarfon. Many artists have painted Dolbadarn castle, not least J. M. W. Turner (1775 – 1851) between 1798 and 1799.

Pass through the gate and follow the path straight ahead to reach a footbridge. Cross this into a car park. Bear right past an information panel and past the children's play area to reach the road at a crossing point. Go straight over and follow the short road up to the High Street. Turn right to the start of the walk.

National Slate Museum

Best Walks in Wales

A series of guide books to take you to every corner of this magnificent walking country

- **Short family walks**
- **Excellent coastal walks**
- **Hill and mountain walks & panoramic views**
- **Level lakeside and valley walks**
- **Woodland and nature walks**
- **Fascinating heritage and history guides**
- **Clear coloured maps**
- **Route photos and attractions on the way**
- **Updated directions**

www.carreg-gwalch.cymru

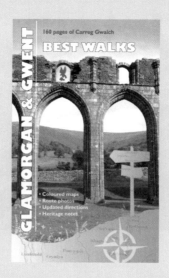